Let Love Find You

Seven Steps to Open Your Heart to love

John Selby

RIDER

LONDON SYDNEY AUCKLAND JOHANNESBURG

3 5 7 9 10 8 6 4 2

Copyright © 2006 John Selby

First published in 2006 by Rider,
an imprint of Ebury Publishing,
Random House,
20 Vauxhall Bridge Road,
London SW1V 2SA

Random House Australia (Pty) Limited
20 Alfred Street, Milsons Point, Sydney,
New South Wales 2061, Australia

Random House New Zealand Limited
18 Poland Road, Glenfield,
Auckland 10, New Zealand

Random House (Pty) Limited
Isle of Houghton, Corner of Boundary Road & Carse O'Gowrie,
Houghton 2198, South Africa

The Random House Group Limited Reg. No. 954009

Papers used by Rider are natural, recyclable products
made from wood grown in sustainable forests.

Printed and bound in Great Britain by
Mackays of Chatham plc, Chatham, Kent

A CIP catalogue record for this book
is available from the British Library

ISBN 9781846040221 (from January 2007)
ISBN 1846040221

Contents

Resources HEART-TO-HEART COMMUNITY

Introduction

How We Come Together

T wo solitary people find themselves standing side by side at the grocery-store checkout stand. Both live alone and yearn for sexual intimacy and a long-term love partner. And indeed, from a wise matchmaker's perspective, these two people might be quite compatible – but unfortunately they stand next to each other, but fail to really tune into each other's presence. The woman has an ideal lover in mind who doesn't at all match this fellow's physical appearance, and besides she's feeling depressed and hardly noticing people around her at all. Meanwhile the man is tense and worrying about a meeting coming up next day at work – he's right then entirely out of touch with his heart and its deeper yearnings.

And so, these two lonely and highly compatible people fail to perceive the other person as a possible intimate companion. Instead of love-at-first-sight ringing bells in their hearts and provoking a bashful but eager conversation, they turn and go their separate solitary ways, chronically yearning for their ideal life partner – while missing one chance after another to fulfil that basic romantic yearning.

This unfortunate scenario happens over and over in the lives of millions of single people. Golden opportunities open up for romantic encounter – but the people involved aren't quite prepared inside their own hearts and minds to perceive the opportunity and act on it.

A few months ago while travelling on a seminar tour, I gave an evening lecture in Zurich and noticed that the majority of people in the audience were young – and most of them had come to the lecture alone. My organizer informed me of a recent lifestyle study showing that 37 per cent of the Zurich population between the ages of 20 and 45 currently live alone as singles, even though most of them feel frustrated and hunger for romantic involvement. As I journeyed to other cities in Europe and the States, I came upon the same situation – a chronic crisis of young (and also not so young) people unable to find sexual fulfilment and lasting relationships.

What is causing this general mating difficulty, and what can be done about it? Relationship experts offer numerous explanations for this epidemic of frustrated singles. They note that traditionally, arranged marriages helped resolve the mating game, with romantic love held secondary to the pragmatics of an economically successful union. But long ago this tradition faded away – leaving young folk (and divorced or widowed older folk as well) to struggle blindly on their own to find a compatible mate.

Many experts blame the media for presenting stereotyped portrayals of idealized romance that programme people's minds with images and expectations that simply don't match everyday lives and possibilities. Single people do all too often hunger for an idealized physical mate, and thus fail to recognize compatible partners because they don't quite match flashy media notions of sexual perfection.

The fear of sexually communicated diseases, combined with anxieties of possible sexual assault and so forth, also tend to keep lonely people at home at night – where there's virtually no hope of romantic encounter. And at work, many people are so consumed in their careers that they're afraid to get caught in a romantic buzz. Even when willing people seeking heart-to-heart contact go out regularly to the night spots that cater to singles, all too often the experience proves discouraging if not downright embarrassing and insulting. Most people in such situations close down their more sensitive presence, armour their hearts and adopt a phoney social image that might lead to casual sex, but doesn't lead any further into serious romance.

And so, after too many heartless sex adventures that led to empty feelings of hopelessness and despair, literally millions of solitary people sit at home at night, watching television or reading books or surfing the internet – doing their best to make it through another lonely evening but all the while yearning for something magical to happen to sweep them off into an idealized romantic encounter.

The Cause of Loneliness – And The Solution

Blaming various external conditions as the cause of our singles crisis might be popular in the press, but ultimately such excuses don't do anything to resolve the dilemma. And the truth is, until just recently we simply didn't have enough scientific and psychological evidence in hand to help us clearly identify the more subtle 'romance variables' that determine if we're actually in optimum position to discover meaningful love. There has also been a dearth of pragmatic programmes teaching how to manage our own minds and emotions, so that we can take control of those variables, and purposefully advance towards deep heart encounter.

A primary purpose of this book is to present, for the first time, newly emerging professional insights into why some people manage to find true love, while so many others continue to live alone and lonely. Most importantly, this text offers readers specific psychological techniques for identifying and then actively resolving each of the 'romance variables' that stands between them and true love.

From my understanding, there are several underlying internal reasons for the inability of so many of us to open our hearts and find a fulfilling sexual partner. First of all, the ingrained habits of our own minds tend to sabotage our potential for opening up to new love. We allow our stream of consciousness to run mostly out of control, fixating either upon mundane survival thoughts and plans, or dwelling overmuch on negative attitudes, apprehensions, prejudices and distortions – that block more positive emotions that would make us attractive to a satisfying partner.

From this new psychological understanding, we continue to live lonely lives mostly because we haven't yet learned to manage our minds properly, so as to heal old emotional wounds, open our hearts and attract a satisfying person into our lives. As we go through each new day, our hearts either drag us down with chronic aching feelings, or we're just mostly numb inside emotionally. Perhaps our parents divorced and left us with a deep unspoken suspicion of romantic love in general. Perhaps we were so wounded in an earlier love affair that we're afraid to ever open up and risk getting hurt again. For whatever reason, all too often we allow negative thoughts and upset emotions to drain our sexual energy – to where we simply aren't all that attractive to potential mates.

The very good news is that learning to transcend such negative inner attitudes and emotions, and prepare our hearts and minds for successful intimate relating, isn't all that mysterious or difficult to accomplish, once the proper mental tools have been applied. This book is designed as a complete programme to teach you how to use such mental tools, and to guide you through each step towards achieving your natural heart-yearnings for sexual intimacy and fulfilment.

Manifesting Your Desired Encounter

Another primary reason so many people haven't yet met their true love is found in the seemingly magical dynamic that suddenly brings two people together in such a way that they instantly recognize each other, and surrender to the magnetic pull of sexual love. This mysterious process that pulls two compatible people towards each other is a process that can be entirely dormant and blocked in a person, or consciously nurtured and activated.

Here's a basic question that arises whenever we consider the seeming magic of two people suddenly finding each other. Is the finding of true love a purely random hit-or-miss phenomenon that we can't really do anything to influence? Are we indeed helpless victims of haphazard chance in the mating game – or does there exist, as most successful couples claim, a certain mysterious magnetism to the process of encountering one's true love?

The answer to this basic question, seen from the perspective of new research into the power of human intent in romantic life, has recently swung away from the victim stance, towards the victor stance. Yes – there is most definitely a great deal we can do, through the employment of effective mind-management techniques, to take control of our romantic lives, prepare ourselves successfully for the desired encounter, and then attract into our lives the special quality of love we hunger for.

Even though millions of lonely people continue to have difficulty in finding satisfying sexual partners and establishing long-term relationships, other people of course do manage to advance to the point where they're ready for successful love – and then experience that desired moment where they come face to face with someone, recognize them somehow as their desired mate . . . and experience love at first sight. What's really happening when two people suddenly turn a corner, look in each other's eyes, recognize each other and surrender to the magnetic pull of romantic encounter? Is there any observable pattern or logic leading up to this moment, any method to the madness of romance?

Fifteen years ago, while living as a single man, I myself experienced a most remarkable three-week period that led up to that one-in-a-million chance encounter with the woman who would become my wife and life partner. Those three weeks preceding my seemingly fated rendezvous were unique in that I happened to be practising a special meditation of regularly observing and recording my inner thoughts and feelings. Being a psychologist, I was able to notice quite clearly, and step by step write down, a definite emotional and attitudinal shift in my thinking habits, which in turn opened my heart to tune into the sudden feeling that I was in contact with my lover – which led to the inner sensation of being guided towards her at some subtle level . . . which finally led to the seemingly random but quite synchronistic beginning of our relationship.

Startled and excited by what I'd discovered in my own singles journey towards union, I sat down and wrote a small book called *Finding Each Other*. Emerging directly from personal experience, it was one of those rare books that just wrote itself, in less than a month – yet remained in print for over ten years, and sold more than fifty thousand copies without really any promotion at all. Clearly, the initial insights I'd been struck with rang resonant bells inside other hearts as well.

Since then, while leading relationship workshops and working with clients in my therapy practice, I've continued to explore and study the phenomenon of romantic encounter, gathering together many true-life accounts of solitary souls suddenly reaching that magical point in their lives where hearts become open, romantic wounds heal, minds and expectations clear, and souls move into what I call attraction-mode.

Based on truly exciting new scientific research on the human mind's power of intent and attraction, my colleagues and I have recently developed a theoretical model demonstrating that it isn't just magic that brings us together. Yes, finding one's true love remains an ultimately mysterious process – but we now understand enough of the underlying attraction process to know how to consciously tap this inner capacity to actively attract and manifest kindred souls into our lives.

Insights From Successful Couples

My inner experience just before I found my own true love was by no means unique – most successful couples that I know have revealed, when questioned, that during the weeks and months leading up to their romantic encounter, several specific realizations and emotional changes happened in their lives – inner mental expansions that can be actively nurtured by anyone hungering for romantic fulfilment.

Successful couples are those in which both partners stay together happily and willingly for a considerable period of time. There are definite inner steps that most successful couples report having moved through, just before their encounter with their new love partner. Here is their advice to you:

• *'Get clear in your mind about who you are seeking . . .'*
A first step that most successful couples mention as preceding their encounter has to do with the remarkable human power of intent. All

too often out of habit and programming, we tend to focus our power of intent towards attaining a fanciful idealistic union with a perfect lover – and this idealistic intent gets in our way of attaining what is actually possible in our lives. There is now solid scientific documentation (from the Princeton Engineering Anomalies Research studies and other experiments) proving that your power of intent does reach out and contact the world around you. So it is vital that you take time to clarify realistically who it is you intend to encounter and live your life with, and make sure that this intent is attainable, as you reach out to contact similarly motivated hearts and minds.

- 'Heal your romantic past . . .'
You aren't going to be ready for new love if you're still feeling wounded by old love. Successful couples report how they first had to finally let go of past romantic disasters, forgive their earlier sexual partners, heal their wounded hearts, and feel good inside their own skins, before new love came their way. The inner step of accepting yourself just as you are, and finding wholeness in your own heart so you no longer feel so emotionally needy, is a major step in preparing for a relationship free from co-dependent tendencies. And I'm sure you'll agree logistically that two people moving through this inner process at the same time are ideally suited to come together in love.

- 'Drop negative attitudes . . .'
Another crucial step in finding true love often involves a change in your attitudes about the kind of person you're seeking. As long as you're looking for your idealized visual image in people you meet, and judging everyone else as not good enough for you, you'll pass by many potential lovers because they don't match your idealized image. When you finally let go your stereotyped dream and open up to people who might not match your programmed ideal, the magic of romance becomes strongly enhanced.

- 'Let yourself feel sexy . . .'
As you begin to feel better inside your heart, to accept and forgive and let go of the past, your sexual charge will begin to feel clear, bright and

powerful – and this expanding sexual charge becomes an actual physical force that empowers your attraction capacity. Successful couples report experiencing a qualitatively different feeling of attractiveness and sexiness in their bodies just before their encounter, which provided them with the confidence and energy to change daily habits, get out more, and put themselves in physical position for a romantic encounter. The specific scientific dynamic of this attraction process remains a partial mystery, but we now know pragmatic ways to encourage this feeling of sexually positive energization in the body.

• *'Use your desire as an emotional magnet . . .'*
In the process of letting go and feeling good in your heart, the inner experience of desire shifts from being a negative aching pain in the heart, to a dynamic positive energy that broadcasts outward – to touch the hearts of other people in similar stages of romantic readiness. As we'll see, there now exists quite exciting scientific verification that the heartfelt power of desire is a measurable force that helps brings two hearts together. So encourage your desire, and learn to focus it outward towards that special person out there also focusing towards you.

• *'Open your heart to receive . . .'*
There is evidence that when their hearts and minds are radiating readiness for sexual encounter and fulfilment, both members approaching a relationship frequently report feeling heart contact with someone 'out there' – who is also aware of them at the same time. We have surprising scientific research showing how this happens, based on the predictions of Albert Einstein, and recently documented for the first time. If you want to fall in love again, you do need to consciously open your heart to receive that person out there who is also looking for you.

• *'Let spontaneity move you . . .'*
Once this sense of 'already being together' happens, the final step towards successful encounter is to surrender fully to the present moment, and allow your feet the freedom to walk in new directions – as each choice of what to do each new moment becomes entrained with the presence of the other person . . . leading to that remarkable

'chance encounter' and instant recognition which really isn't pure chance, but guided by subtle forces we're just beginning to understand and use to our advantage.

The Heart – Open To Receive

Scientific insights surely help to understand the mysteries of romantic attraction and encounter. But ultimately the mystery remains greater than our present scientific method can fathom, and we find that our primary guide towards true love is still the direct experience happening inside our own hearts. In this book, I'd like first of all to share with you new research that shows that the heart is vastly more than just an organic pump – in fact, scientists at NYU and other universities are now talking about the heart being 'the fifth brain'. We can in fact seek wisdom and guidance from our own hearts, and also learn to speak from our hearts.

But all too often when we're alone and lonely, we tend to constantly fill our minds with negative thoughts and emotions, and keep our hearts fixated upon upsetting memories, depressing attitudes, and aching emotions. One of the great tragedies from this point of view is that as long as we're constantly caught up in our own negative thoughts and feelings, we're stuck in what I call broadcast mode – sending out over and over our inner cry for communion and contact.

The dilemma that we'll address in this book is this: that all the while we're thinking up a storm inside our minds and are all stirred up emotionally from our chronic worries and imaginations, we never shift into what I call 'receive mode' – where our minds become quiet, our emotions calm, and our hearts therefore able to open up and tune into the presence of like-minded people reaching out to us. Because of all our inner mental agitations and heart constrictions, we're simply not available to be touched by another heart.

This is one of the reasons I've titled this book *Let Love Find You* – because a primary missing variable in the mating game, as I see it, is the regular conscious shifting of our hearts and minds from noisy active broadcast mode, to quiet open-to-receive mode. To transcend this situation, we'll devote an entire chapter to learning how to quiet our thoughts, calm our emotions, and open our hearts to the inflow of love.

I clearly remember being alone one night, practising a basic 'opening to receive' technique I'd been developing for spiritual purposes. I had recently finally reached a point in my own emotional healing where I'd recovered from my previous romantic fiasco, and was feeling very good in my heart even when alone. I'd also discovered at long last that I could be my own best friend, and feel love in my heart even when alone. Therefore my heart was singing a happy tune that evening, even though I was surely hoping to someday find true love.

And so, having recently moved through several of the emotional-healing steps I'll be guiding you through, I was sitting there focusing on a beautiful meditation to allow spiritual love in general to flow into my heart – and suddenly, as I was quietly holding my heart in receive mode, I became vibrantly aware . . . of a very specific person's presence – right inside my own heart.

I was so jolted that I snapped out of the meditation, wondering what had happened. It took me a few moments to get up the nerve to move back into the meditation – and sure enough, when I entered into that receptive heart space, I again became aware of a special person's loving presence in my heart.

Over the next three weeks, I would regularly return to this meditation and tune into this sense of being in contact with someone out there who was also tuned into my presence . . . and through trusting and surrendering to this new feeling and power of attraction in my heart, I was able to set myself free, open up to spontaneous changes in my daily routine – to where ultimately, yes, I opened a door and there she was . . .

Balancing Mastery and Mystery

Even now as I reflect on my own experience of the radical process that brought me together with the love of my life, I find myself wondering how much of that process can be explained through scientific logic, and how much of the process of falling in love remains a mystery – where forces greater than the human mind can grasp come into play to bring us together in love.

Yes, we can manage our minds to our romantic advantage, and consciously move beyond the psychological inhibitions that stand between us and true love. But throughout this book, I'll also be encouraging you to temporarily let go of your thinking mind's limited grip on reality, so you can surrender to the deeper attractive forces that will help guide you to the love you're seeking.

In this light, quite openly, the programmes in this book do have a spiritual dimension to them, specifically because science only takes us so far into the mystery of love and intimacy. However, it's in no way necessary for the success of these programmes to believe any particular religious theology about God or Universal Consciousness or whatever you might call the higher unifying force of the universe. This book ultimately is not about beliefs and concepts of the thinking mind – it's about actual experiences that you know are valid, because you feel them in your heart.

The bottom line is this – you are blessed with a thinking mind that has great power, when freed from negative attitudes and expectations. You are also blessed with a deep-feeling heart that has great power, when freed from emotional wounds and contractions. And your true capacity to manifest the lover you so desire becomes activated when you learn to bring mind and heart together – this is the crucial step you'll be mastering here, the step that turns your chronic yearning into a genuine attractive force, that will allow true love find you.

You are a single person seeking to find and team up with that one perfect person out there who is your ideal mate. My observation and understanding of life is that there are actually quite a number of potential life mates for you out there, fully compatible people who are searching for someone just like you. When you let go of 'the one ideal soul mate' and open to the reality that there are many people out there who can satisfy your deep longings for intimate mating, you expand your encounter opportunity greatly.

You Are Already Together

By the laws of logic, if you are destined to meet someone at some point in the future, from the greater scientific overview you are in fact already on perfect course for that encounter. Yes, over and over again you will pass by someone who could have been your ideal lover, because one or both of you weren't quite ready for the encounter. But at some point you are going to coincide with someone – and even right now in this present moment, you are on target with that person, and therefore connected with that person.

Holding this ultimate certainty in mind, as your next breaths come and go and the moments standing between you and your new love effortlessly become fewer and fewer, you can choose to just relax – and enjoy your inevitable flow towards encounter and union. During the next weeks and perhaps months while you actively learn to take charge of your mind and deal with the variables that you can influence, you can also ease up and trust that the variables you can't influence are naturally working to your advantage.

Many of you have read my earlier books on mind management, showing how you can take control of your thoughts and beliefs, and generate the life you truly want to live. This new 'romantic-encounter' programme takes that general approach to managing your life to your advantage, and focuses these mental tools on the specific intent of overcoming the inner obstacles that stand between you and the natural process of attracting, contacting, and encountering your intimate mate.

As I mentioned before, there are hundreds, perhaps thousands of like-minded people out there – any one of whom can bring you lasting satisfaction as a life partner. Who knows which one of these people will be the one you're destined to meet and team up with. But from here onward, you no longer have to sit alone feeling helpless at night, or hang out in a lonely crowd aching in your heart with the throes of loneliness and isolation.

Instead, you can now choose to regularly go into action with enjoyable exercises and meditations that will prepare your heart and mind for satisfying love. You are no longer a victim – you have at hand the needed set of mental tools for actively succeeding, step by step, with your heart's most important challenge.

Furthermore, you are no longer alone – right now, the person you're going to meet and fall in love with sometime in the future is already out there, looking for you, anticipating the coming encounter just as much as you are. This book is very much all about tuning into this person right now, so that even before you come physically together for the first time, you are already communing heart-to-heart. Carrying this sense of already being together in your hearts will make the process of finding each other so much easier and more enjoyable!

Manage Your Romantic Mind

The core to success with the Selby Attraction Method lies in your ability to manage your mind however you choose to. Rather than continuing to let your romantic life run mostly on automatic, I'm going to teach you how to manage your mind so that you regularly turn your focus of attention in the specific directions that will optimize and indeed activate your romantic experience.

We'll start this process very gently in chapter one, by learning easy ways to shift your mind's attention away from all your chronic bothersome feelings of loneliness, hopelessness and confusion, towards good feelings in your body. You'll be surprised at how easy it actually is, with a bit of guidance, to encourage an enjoyable rush of pleasure and well-being throughout your body, and especially in your heart.

We'll then begin to explore your old attitudes about your ideal lover, and expand those attitudes so that you are wide open to all potential lovers similar enough to you to create a long-term fulfilling relationship. We'll also consider your heart's emotional contractions and wounds from previous affairs, and move through a healing process that will enable you to forgive and let go of old relationships, and open up to love yourself – just as you are. And once you learn to enter into and broadcast a bright, expansive, self-sufficient presence, we'll move into the action-phase where you employ the new scientific understandings of your mind's power of intent, and actively open your heart to attract your desired lover.

I'm well aware that this book will challenge you considerably as you expose and explore your innermost feelings, achings, yearnings and uncertainties. I promise that each step of the way, I'll provide you with excellent mental and emotional tools to successfully heal old heart wounds and negative mental habits, as you come to love yourself more, and open your heart to others who will love you just as you are.

And so, let's move right on to the actual programmes. Please feel free to also visit our Let Love Find You website at www.johnselby.com if you want further guidance through the programmes, plus the opportunity to meet kindred souls online who are also working with this programme, and ready to meet you. Throughout, hold in mind that there's plenty of time here, there's no rush. After all, your initial preparation for love will determine the success of future encounters. So grant yourself relaxed timeframes to enjoy each step of this process . . . as you prepare your heart and soul fully for the love it so desires.

BEGINNING REFLECTIONS

Each of the chapters in this book will end with a specific suggestion, technique or meditation that you'll want to reflect upon, experience, and perhaps learn by heart as you develop your own daily programme for attracting love into your life. To end this introduction, I'd like to share with you ten vital psychological premises that will fuel your success in finding true love. Please read each of these in turn, and for each, pause and reflect upon your own present understanding of the premise. Do you agree with the statement? And as you pause with each statement for a few breaths, what thoughts come to you . . .?

1. *Where you focus your power of attention determines what happens in your life . . .*

Each new moment, you are determining your fate based on what you're thinking about, where you're holding your mind's focus, and in general, how you're managing your own mind. This question of where you're focusing your attention moment-to-moment becomes crucial in romance, because all too often people have mental and emotional habits that directly inhibit their ability to attract and locate a compatible partner – because they simply aren't focusing in the right directions. So . . . are you ready to take conscious control of where you focus your mind's attention?

2. Your sexual power is the underlying energetic charge for attracting love . . .

Your body is both electrical and magnetic in nature, as science demonstrates – and your moment-to-moment management of your sexual energy determines your power-capacity for contacting and attracting like-minded people to you. Are you ready to learn how to purify and amplify your sexual charge, so as to powerfully attract love into your life?

3. At any given moment, there are a large number of potential mates available . . .

The notion that there is only one person in the entire world who will make a successful mate for you is simply false – and needs to be discarded. There are surely hundreds, even thousands of people with whom you can successfully relate and even mate for a lifetime. Therefore the reality is this: you're not trying to attract and meet just one person in the world – you're reaching out to contact all compatible people who are likewise reaching out to people like you. Are you ready to open up to all compatible people out there, so that you have many available options?

4. Your power of intent does touch others – if you direct it properly . . .

Your mind's power of intent, as recently proven scientifically, can broadcast outward and be received by other minds, quite beyond the confines of space and time. You can learn specific mind-management meditations that enable you to clarify your romantic intent, so that the broadcast you send out to the world is clean of old attitudes and emotions, and resonant with an intent that like-minded folk will respond to. Are you ready to learn how to direct your power of intent thusly?

5. *Your heart broadcasts and receives – you can establish heart contact from afar . . .*

Research demonstrates that your heart is a massive broadcast-receive system that can tune into compatible broadcasts – and generate the inner feeling of being connected, even before the moment of physical sensory encounter. Are you ready to prepare your heart for positive powerful broadcasting of your personality, presence, your intent, and your yearnings?

6. *You must shift into receive mode, to truly make contact heart to heart . . .*

Almost all of the time, most of us are in broadcast mode, thinking thinking thinking. The Selby Attraction Method will teach you how to regularly quiet your mind, quiet the heart broadcast – so that you shift into receive mode, and allow other people to reach out and discover you! This is how to consciously let love find you: pause, be quiet – and in the present moment, experience who is out there, seeking you. Are you ready to become vulnerable, and let like-minded people actually come to you energetically, and touch you with their love, their hunger, and their presence?

7. *You must heal your own heart, before you can succeed in new love . . .*

All of us have been wounded in love earlier in our lives. Until we practise the principles of mind management and consciously accept, forgive and let go of past romantic conflicts, we can't open our hearts to new love. Actively encouraging emotional healing is a vital part of the Selby Attraction Method. Are you ready to remember . . . forgive . . . heal and let go of old relationship wounds?

8. When you are no longer emotionally needy, you are ready for new love . . .

All too often, we seek out a sexual partner because we feel empty inside and want someone else to make us feel whole. Mature love that nurtures lasting relationships begins with self-love. Right when you reach the point of feeling good inside your own skin, and happy with your own company, you attain that perfect state for broadcasting to, contacting and encountering a person equally whole. This inner wholeness is the foundation for lasting love – and this book will help you actively nurture the progression towards self-love and inner peace. Are you ready for a major shift in your sense of who you are – away from being an emotionally needy person, to being an emotionally whole person on your own, with or without a life partner?

9. The basic Attraction Meditation needs to be done at least once a day . . .

The Selby Method is a whole-life technique for becoming personally content and emotionally healthy – as preparation for success in the romantic hunt. The seven-step preparation and attraction meditation you'll be learning in this book needs to be done regularly, in order for inner healing to take place, and mind-management techniques to be mastered. This meditation is a pleasure to move through, and also will rapidly evoke inner growth and awakening to your deeper powers and potential. Your mate will appear as if by magic, specifically because you're adequately prepared for that encounter. Are you feeling ready to both read this book, and set aside time each day to actively prepare yourself for true love?

10. You can't make love come to you – but you can allow it to find you . . .

At the same time that you are seeking true love, there are like-minded people out there, seeking you. Once you make heart contact with someone 'out there', the two of you begin a veritable dance as you make one choice after another, that ultimately leads you into that moment of physical congruency and encounter. You can't force this coming encounter. You can only remain in receive mode, and allow love to find you. Are you ready to fully commit to a new way of finding love, in which you give up manipulating your romantic life, and instead, surrender to participating in the deeper magic of love?

Even before we begin our formal training programme for letting love find you, see what happens right now when you pause for a few moments . . . tune into your breathing . . . your heart . . . your yearnings . . . and see if you can feel someone out there . . . also yearning to meet you . . .

pause . . . breathe . . . reflect . . . experience

Part One

SEVEN STEPS TO FINDING EACH OTHER

Chapter 1

Clarify Your Primary Yearnings

HEART ENCOUNTER – ONE

Lesley had been living with a girlfriend from work for seven months or so, ever since her last relationship painfully broke apart. During those seven difficult months she'd managed to recover from the aching pain of her lost love, and had recently been feeling actually quite good in her heart, even a bit sexy one particular late-afternoon when she got off the bus and headed up the five-minute walk to her apartment. Here's how she describes the next few minutes:

There was a wind blowing that evening, it was cold and I was hurrying to get home – but I was also feeling invigorated by the walking. One of the guys at work had flirted with me at lunch and that'd felt good, so I guess I was feeling a bit sexy as I walked along the street, thinking of taking a hot bath when I got home.

Some guy my age was walking down the street towards me and at first I didn't pay him any attention. But as he got closer I thought I recognized him, he looked strangely familiar although I couldn't place the face. I slowed down as we approached each other, and he did too. For no reason my heart started pounding loud in my chest and I felt slightly dizzy, like I needed to stop and catch my breath even though the hill wasn't all that steep.

We walked past each other and our eyes met for just a very short time – and then he was gone and I was walking on up the street . . . but the intense look in his eyes had penetrated my soul so strongly that I found myself stopping and turning around in his direction – and I found him doing just the same thing, standing there looking at me.

I remember the sound of the wind in my ears, whipping my hair into my face, and for a moment I felt such a rising charge of intense emotion, or yearning, that I wanted to run away. He started walking towards me, and rather than run away, I took a few steps in his direction as if we were being physically pulled together – until we were standing quite close to each other, face to face. And what did we do? Nothing. We just stood there, we can't remember for how long, and continued looking into each other's eyes . . . because pow – there was no question, this was him, history being made – my guy!

If you look back to when you first saw the title of this book, you'll probably remember that you felt certain inner emotions and yearnings that made you then reach out and take the book in your hands. And right now, some inner motivation within you has moved you to spend time with the book. Let's begin our Let Love Find You journey by looking directly at the underlying intent and pressure you feel inside you, which is pushing you to devote precious time and attention in the direction of this book and the programmes herein.

Just by being born a human being on this earth, you carry within you a whole array of emotional needs and yearnings that will push you towards fulfilment throughout your life. It's important to realize that you're not the only one feeling as you do – each and every one of us gets up each and every day with the same basic emotional hungers to be accepted by our family, friends and community. We also yearn to be able to share our inner feelings with someone who lovingly respects who we are. Furthermore we desire to make intimate physical contact with at least one heartful person who welcomes our warm hugs and friendship, and responds with similar loving feelings and actions.

Furthermore we all have even more intimate hungers to regularly express our sexual desires through putting aside all inhibitions and plunging into full-blown erotic interaction with someone we find attractive sexually, and who feels the same way about us. I hope you'll allow me to speak openly about even this deepest dimension of your romantic desires, so that we can get right to the heart of what you need to satisfy the yearning that presently pushes you to read this book and see what you can do to fulfil your romantic desires.

When I use the word 'romantic' I am not speaking of the sappy and often totally phoney romance portrayed in romance novels and magazines. For me romance is a very precious, real quality of the human soul, where we surrender to feelings and desires that underlie the very foundation of family and society. Genuine romance is a fire of love burning brightly in our lives, hopefully throughout long and deeply rewarding relationships all the way to the end of our stay on earth. Romance in a very real sense is what makes life worth living – it's the core of good feelings and love that blossom into successful families, magnificent art, and even spiritual awakening.

So the yearning to find romance in life is, for me and I hope for you as well, a most noble and beautiful and worthwhile yearning that surely should be front-centre on your list of needs to fulfil.

Feeling Your Romantic Yearnings

So often when clients first come to me seeking psychological or spiritual counselling, they complain that they're suffering from depression, or chronic worrying, or an inability to sleep at night, or difficulty concentrating at work. Often they come in complaining about how their parents or friends, boss or lover are making them suffer – and how unfairly the world is mistreating them. Quite often they blame themselves for all their inner anguish, saying they're inadequate, that they're hopeless failures in life and have given up the fight to help themselves.

But almost always their real complaint, once they begin to get clear on their inner feelings and disappointments with life, begins to centre around the simple fact that right at the core of their being, they feel alone, lonely, unloved and unlovable. Almost never have I had a potential client come to my office seeking psychological help who felt well loved and able to love deeply. And almost always when people come to me seeking help, they lack a primary sexual partner who loves them just as they are, and serves as a true best friend.

Furthermore, to be honest, most clients recover and heal and blossom in life only when they have learned to admit to their heart's deepest desires and yearnings, and then mastered the fine art of opening their hearts to love, and finding a successful sexual partner who in essence takes my place as primary friend and confidant. Many therapy techniques spend year after year with a client analyzing the past and trying to form giant new concepts of what life is all about. But very often, the core need of the client to clarify and satisfy his or her primary heart yearnings isn't directly addressed, nor resolved.

I assume as I write this book that you have come to me seeking the fast track to finding true love. This means I'm not going to load this book with complex concepts about romance and sexual yearnings and fulfilment – rather we're going to keep the focus strongly on you and what you're feeling right now as you read this book. And we're going to identify your own inner pressures that right now are pushing you into action – and use those inner energies to generate the healing, insights and action that will bring your yearnings to the point of satisfaction.

So as a first step, let's begin by turning your mind's focus of attention directly towards your inner feelings. I don't mean this as an intellectual exercise – what I'm suggesting (and will continue to do so throughout this book) is that you begin to clearly look at what feelings are under pressure inside you, begging for satisfaction. Your yearnings aren't just abstractions, they're actual energy. And that energy is what we'll tap, to actually accomplish your romantic goals. The challenge is in identifying the emotional energy, purifying it, and then applying it in the proper directions that will bear romantic fruit. Let's jump in by focusing on your breathing, because in truth, all your feelings and desires are centred in your breathing experience – you feel and express your yearnings through your breathing, so this is the best place to focus, to come to the core of your motivation:

Even as you continue reading these words, allow these words to begin to point your mind's attention in directions that will shed light on what's really going on inside you. Gently begin to turn your full sensory attention to the actual feeling of the air flowing in and out your nose as your breaths come and go . . . make no effort to breathe . . . just experience the sensation coming to your awareness, of the air flowing in . . . and flowing out . . . and flowing in again . . .

Now while you continue to pay attention to the sensation of the air flowing in and out your nose (or mouth), expand your sensory awareness so that you are also aware of the feelings of movement in your chest, and your belly, as each breath comes and goes . . . again make no effort to breathe . . . let your breathing stop when it wants to . . . experience being empty of air . . . and let your next breath come totally on its own . . . as you focus on the actual experience happening all the time, caused by your natural breathing.

Pause for a few breaths, close your eyes if you want to, and fully tune into the actual experience of your breathing . . . notice if your breathing is tense, or relaxed – enjoyable, or somehow caught in a bothersome feeling . . .

pause . . . breathe . . . reflect . . . experience

Going To The Heart

Tuning into your breathing is almost always the best first step for anything related to your feelings and yearnings, because as we mentioned before, your emotions are expressed through your changes in breathing, and through the sounds and words you generate which are, of course, also a product of your breathing. How you are breathing at any given moment is always a direct indicator of how you are feeling – and to become regularly aware of your breathing is to bring yourself deeply in touch with your feelings . . . so that you can then do something about them if they're bothering you, or fully enjoy them if they're a pleasure.

However, in the work I do, there's another vital expansion of consciousness to learn to do regularly, beyond just breath awareness. What you accomplish when you tune into the sensation of the air flowing in and out your nose (go ahead and do it again!) and then expand your awareness to include the movements in your chest and belly as you breathe, is really quite remarkable – you shift your entire experience from your usual constant flow of thoughts in your head, down to your nose, and then on down into your chest and belly. Breath awareness instantly moves you from thought, into feelings – and once you're focused down in the chest and belly experiencing the sensations of movement in your torso, you're quite effortlessly in position to expand your awareness another notch – to include your heart, right in the middle of your breathing.

Often one of the most difficult things to do for someone who's suffering from loneliness or lack of a fulfilling sexual relationship is to turn attention directly to the heart. Why? Because the heart is chronically aching, and who wants to focus on the agony of the heart? Much better to never focus down there in the heart region, where there's so much pain – right?

Wrong. If there's one thing that feels worse than the aching of a lonely heart, it's not being in touch with your heart at all. So many many people tend to do just this – they numb their hearts, they develop the mental habit of constantly being fixated in their heads and in their thoughts, so that they can avoid the pain they find in their hearts. Unfortunately what they accomplish with this negative mind management is a plunge into the Hades of no feelings at all – which feels like being dead even while still alive, which of course is the ultimate terrible suffering.

So, over and over in this book, I'm going to gently suggest that you begin to develop the mind-management habit of returning your mind's focus of attention down to your heart region, so that there's the potential for healing to happen in your heart, and then the attraction process which will bring new love into your heart and life. Trust that as I bring your attention down to your heart, I won't just leave you fixated on the negative feelings that hurt. We'll quickly begin to learn new ways to manage your mind that encourage change and growth and healing – and the inflow of love into your heart.

In a moment I'm going to guide you through this simple but dramatic process of looking directly into your heart, and feeling whatever emotions you find there. We're going to look in such a way that you'll be able to begin to clarify exactly what it is that you hunger for in life – so that you can then begin the process of activating your inner power of intent, to manifest that which you hunger for. Intent is everything here – it's the driving force that generates the inner action that step by step generates the manifestation of your dream. First, let's find out what that dream is, and advance it consciously so that it's a dream you can truly fulfil. Here we go – just walk through it gently so that you begin to get the lie of the land. Hold in mind that each time you move through this process, you'll have a new experience. And each new experience will be what you're ready to confront and explore, right now:

As you read these words, allow your mind's attention to shift so that it's focused on the sensory experience happening in your nose as you breathe . . . make no effort to breathe . . . set your breathing free to stop . . . and to start again . . . and as you feel the air flowing in and out your nose (or mouth), expand your awareness to also include the sensory experience of the movements in your chest, and in your belly – all at the same time!

And now, as you remain aware of your whole breathing experience, effortlessly allow your awareness to expand so that you're also aware of the feelings in your heart, right in the middle of your breathing . . .

Don't try to change anything . . . just experience your breaths coming and going . . . allow your breathing to slow down and deepen on its own . . . and right in the middle of your breathing, be aware of how your heart feels right now . . . breathe into that feeling . . . allow it to change or stay the same . . . just experience how you feel in your heart right now, for the next five or ten breaths . . .

pause . . . breathe . . . reflect . . . experience

Your Heart Quiz

As you stay aware of the feelings in your heart, let me ask you a few questions that might help you to clarify exactly what it is you're missing in your life that would allow your heart to sing rather than yearn. Try reading the first question below, then tune into your breathing and slowly read the question again – then close your eyes and say to yourself, 'Yes,' if this is true, or 'No' if it isn't true. In the process of expressing your response to the question, you'll feel in your heart if the quality mentioned in the question is important to you. Of course, you can say yes or no to more than one question . . .

As you explore these seven questions, remember that breath awareness is the direct path to your heart – so before moving on to the next question, be sure to again turn your attention to the air flowing in and out your nose . . . expand your awareness to include the movements in your chest and belly as you breathe . . . and expand your awareness to include the feeling in your heart, as you do this beginning the heart quiz:

Question 1: Are you yearning to regain a love relationship you have lost?

Question 2: Do you hunger to find a new lover and life mate?

Question 3: Are you yearning to find someone to be your best friend?

Question 4: Is finding a fulfilling sexual partner something you desire strongly?

Question 5: Are you hungering for someone to feel close to emotionally?

Question 6: Do you seek a marital partner to create a family with?

Question 7: Are you hungering for a spiritual mate to live with for life?

This seemingly simple quiz can actually be very powerful if you allow it to help you penetrate to the centre of your inner hungers for romantic fulfilment. Now, let's ask your heart specifically, related to the feelings evoked by the above questions: what sort of person you seek, in order to break beyond your present unsatisfied feelings. Again, take time to hold your awareness centred in your breathing and heart – and breathe into whatever thoughts and feelings arise . . .

Which of the following qualities do you seek in a sexual partner? For instance, say to yourself, 'Yes, I seek an intelligent partner . . .' if this is true – or otherwise say to yourself, 'Being intelligent isn't an important quality to me . . .'

a. ____ intelligent
b. ____ sexy
c. ____ spiritual
d. ____ loving
e. ____ funny
f. ____ friendly
g. ____ forgiving
h. ____ patient
i. ____ clean
j. ____ athletic
k. ____ philosophical
l. ____ mature
m. ____ likes kids
n. ____ successful

Again, this list isn't just a one-time read – if you want to discover more clearly who it is you want in your life, you'll want to spend some devoted time reflecting on each of the above qualities, so that you gain clarity about the importance of each.

How About Your Own Qualities?

Okay now, to be fair – let's see what happens when you perceive yourself by the same qualities you just established for your new lover. What I'm trying to get at here, is a realistic sense of who you are, who you want to bring into your life, and how well these two concepts you hold in your mind match each other. This is such an important process to go through, because all too often, we tend to hold ideal images in our minds of who we want to become lovers with – and if we're holding unrealistic images in our minds of who we're seeking, we surely won't, in reality, find such a person who will also be interested in us.

Everyone tends to carry forward into their present lives, attitudes and concepts developed earlier in life. We were conditioned as children and young adults with the attitudes and beliefs of our parents and community. We were also strongly conditioned by the media regarding the ideal life mate, sexual partner, and so forth. I want to help you identify your prevailing attitudes and assumptions about who you think will satisfy you as a sexual partner – and then encourage you to modify and alter and advance your image of who you're seeking towards an attainable, realistic sense of that person.

Otherwise as you go through the next days and weeks and months seeking true love, you're liable to look the real thing right in the face and not recognize it, because your eyes and heart and mind are looking for something else. We tend to see what we're looking for, and to miss everything else. And what a deep shame, even a tragedy it is, when two highly compatible people meet, yet reject each other because they don't match their inner image of what they're looking for.

So again, here's the same list that you used to determine the qualities that are important in the person you're looking for. It's fairly obvious that if you want these qualities in your lover, your lover is going to want similar qualities in you. If you're looking for somebody who's really sexy, and you're not – what's going to happen? If you're not so smart or interested in philosophy, are you going to satisfy someone who is? Let's get real honest here, because only honesty will move you into the deep rewarding relationship you seek.

How do you rate yourself on the following scales? Say something like this to yourself, for each quality: 'Yes, I'm very smart,' or perhaps, 'Well, I'm not such a super-intelligent person.' And again, first tune into your breathing, and the feelings in your heart, so that when you speak this statement, you're speaking honestly from your own heart – and allow this process to be an act of self-discovery!

a. _____ intelligent (are you, and should this matter – etc)
b. _____ sexy
c. _____ spiritual
d. _____ loving
e. _____ funny
f. _____ friendly
g. _____ forgiving
h. _____ patient
i. _____ clean
j. _____ athletic
k. _____ philosophical
l. _____ mature
m. _____ likes kids
n. _____ successful

pause . . . breathe . . . reflect . . . experience

Your Self-Image

Hopefully you're beginning to bring to mind all sorts of assumptions and notions you hold in your mind from past conditionings, about who you are and who you want for your romantic partner. Let's now go another step with this process because you'll find it invaluable in loosening up your ability to attract a truly compatible person into your life. Obviously if you're not compatible with someone, the relationship won't last. So let's play a visualization game, and see how your image of your ideal lover evolves.

Right now, you hold mostly unconsciously in your mind a visual self-image of what you look like to others – which is sometimes overly idealistic, and sometimes overly mean to yourself. It's amazing how some people go around thinking that they're much more physically sexy and attractive than other people see them, for instance, while others go around thinking that they're much less pleasing to the eye than they actually are. How about you?

The first step here is to honestly envision how you look to other people when you walk into a room. Let's do this little guided visualization process, and see what you see.

After reading through this paragraph, I request that you close your eyes . . . tune into your breathing . . . your heart . . . and, effortlessly, imagine you're in a living room somewhere, and the door to the room opens. You look to the door, and in walks – yourself! What do you look like? As you walk into the room and stand there, what is your posture? What is your expression? Are you sexy or drab? Are you friendly, or not? How do you appear, to other people – look, imagine, see!

pause . . . breathe . . . reflect . . . experience

Upgrading Your Self-Image

Once you've fully experienced in your own mind's eye what you look like, ask yourself if that inner vision is actually realistic – are you as beautiful or ugly as you envisioned yourself? If you want, take time now to go get recent photos of you, or look at yourself in the mirror. What do you really look like? Please, take time with this, and over the next days begin to explore how you feel towards your own self.

Especially, begin to be honest about how you feel towards yourself. Throughout this book we'll be exploring various ways in which you might tend, for instance, to put yourself down as less attractive than you are, or than you can be. As a psychologist sometimes I want to just scream out loud at the constant media barrage we're all being conditioned by, as television presents us with idealized physical bodies that we then mostly unconsciously begin to assume we must match ourselves, in order to be attractive to other people.

The reality is that 99 per cent of us don't in any way have the genetics of the models and actors we see on television or in the movies. Yet as we allow ourselves to be programmed by the media with these idealized bodies, we tend to judge ourselves by those impossible standards – and also to judge our potential sexual partners by the same impossible standards of sexual prowess. Here and now in this discussion, we need to actively begin to throw off such unrealistic conditioning, and learn to love ourselves and those around us based not on media programming, but on the feelings in our hearts.

For instance, when you imagined yourself walking in through that door, how did you feel – did you love your own shape and presence just as it is, or did you judge it as somehow not sexy enough? Take a deep breath . . . bring that self-image back to mind for a moment, and be honest – how do you judge yourself on the sexy scale?

My job here isn't to condition you in my own particular directions regarding how you look. Certainly if you want to be attractive sexually, it's a good idea not to over-eat, and to exercise regularly. If you want to find a realistic match, chances are you're going to end up with someone who's in about the same shape as you are – so it's your choice whether to stay out of shape and find a similarly out-of-shape person to team up with, or to get in better shape and end up with someone in similar condition.

Here's the truth as I see it – we all come into this world with our particular genetic inheritance that by and large determines our looks. The media conditions us to believe that people with more sexy genes have more pleasure sexually, and enjoy life in general more than people who weren't blessed with physically ideal genes and bodies – but this just isn't true. Quite the contrary, a great many physically attractive people end up in therapy specifically because their good looks are almost a curse for them. Having an ideal build does not in any way guarantee sexual and emotional success in a lasting meaningful relationship.

In the opposite direction, a great many people who are far less than media-perfect physically, experience remarkable sexual pleasure and enduring intimacy with equally less-than-media-perfect mates. Physical beauty just isn't a factor in quality of orgasm and depth of heart intimacy – unless you get hung up on thinking it is.

So for all of us who are less than physically perfect according to the media, we have the choice of either feeling ugly and going around projecting ugly vibes – or accepting our unique physical presence and going around projecting our own version of sexual beauty. You right now have that choice. And your romantic future depends on your taking time to explore that choice in the next days and weeks, and making the choice that liberates you from the media rather than keeps you victimized by it.

Just see what comes to mind, when you rate yourself based on the following criteria – how do you judge yourself on each quality, and is your judgment fair or harsh on your own self?

Quite often I feel . . .

___ sexy	___ enthusiastic
___ ugly	___ weak
___ depressed	___ lonely
___ witty	___ attractive
___ angry	___ lost
___ inspired	___ clever
___ anxious	___ sad
___ lazy	___ fat
___ successful	___ satisfied
___ confused	___ worthless
___ hopeful	___ trusting

You And Your New Lover

Let's focus specifically on physical looks right now. You probably agree that people of similar physical condition tend to attract each other and form lasting unions. Sometimes yes, physical qualities don't matter at all in a relationship – beauty and the beast do once in a while mate up and succeed in that relationship wonderfully. But usually if you look at couples walking down the street together, you'll notice that they are fairly well matched physically. People do tend to team up with people who are similar to them – that's what compatibility is all about.

So I challenge you, if you are one of the many people who hold an impossibly beautiful or handsome image in your mind of who you're seeking as a life mate, to let go of that impossible image. This is important to do, if you want to find the fully possible real person out there who's just right for you. To hell with perfection. Away with idealized beauty. Enough of painfully handsome models with their starving expressions – begin to create in your mind a realistic image of who you are, and who you'll be compatible with. Otherwise loneliness will be your constant companion, rather than a real-life loving person. Are you ready to make this step? Are you ready to give up ideal images and embrace a real and highly compatible dream lover – in the flesh?

In this regard – and I don't mean to get overly personal here – most people living without a regular sexual partner do tend to masturbate. And of course we tend to do this either while looking at idealized media images on the web or wherever, or while dreaming in our minds of the most sexy erotic partner to stimulate our private fantasy and sexual excitement . . . yes, this is what we tend to do. And there's nothing wrong with holding idealized images of sexy people in our minds to provoke our solitary sexual release.

But if the long-term aim here is to move beyond sexual solitude and prepare ourselves for real-life sexual mating with a compatible real-life body and heart and soul, we must consciously put aside all our idealized images of our dream lover – and begin to open up to someone who isn't perfect, who in fact is no more sexy than we are. Such an act of acceptance of reality, even a wholehearted embrace of reality, is the only path to true sexual fulfilment. We must accept ourselves and our sexual partner just the way we are, if we're to surrender to total sexual passion and erogenous fulfilment. Do you agree with this? And is this important for you?

Consider how your eyes move and what they look at, when you're out around town. Are you looking mostly at the handsome or beautiful people you encounter, and hoping somehow that you'll maybe someday be able to take them to bed and bring them into your heart? Are you constantly, and mostly unconsciously, judging all the people with other-than-perfect bodies as not worthy of your attention? Please over the next days and weeks begin to notice your habits of perception in public. Later we'll get specific about how to change your perceptual habits when out around town, so that you're able to let go of old ideal-istic seeking patterns, and thus become able to recognize realistic possibilities when they present themselves to you. For now, just begin to be self-aware when in public – and observe your existing visual habits. That very process of observing your habits in action will help them to begin to evolve in more successful directions.

Okay, in this light here's another visualization to do several times in the next weeks. Each time be open to a new experience, as your self image and the image of your lover continue to evolve. With a sense of humour, first imagine your ideal lover if you want to – and see how you look standing with this person . . . and each time you do this visualization, allow your ideal lover to look more and more in the same ballpark as you:

After reading this paragraph, imagine you're in a room. A door opens and two people walk into the room – you and your new lover. You stand together, chatting with your host. Imagination whatever partner you feel comfortable standing next to. Considering your own physical presence, what sort of person in general is going to feel comfortable as your partner . . . allow this image to evolve to where you feel good about yourself, and good about your partner . . .

pause . . . breathe . . . reflect . . . experience

Stating Your Intent

So here you are, reading onward in this book after having reflected a bit on who you're hungering to meet and team up with, and what you want to accomplish in your life romance-wise. I hope you'll return to the exercises in this chapter a number of times in the next days and weeks, so that you advance further into clarity. Hold in mind that this isn't a book that you just read through and put aside. You're learning exercises that often need to be moved through several times, to have their full effect. You might also want to go online for the audio guidance available at www.singles.johnselby.com.

I fully understand your eagerness and downright impatience to move fast through this preparation period that will ultimately climax in your impending romantic encounter. At the same time, from loads of experience in guiding people through this process, I can say four definite things: first, preparing does take time; second, you will enjoy each step of the preparation phase; third, your success with the new relationship may very well depend upon spending enough time in preparation, to be ready for success in the relationship.

My fourth point is this: your success with this 'finding each other' process will be strongly influenced by the particular clarity of intent that you bring to the challenge at hand. So let's take a look at your present intentions here, and give you room to advance and clarify your intent as needed.

See how you feel when you say the following 'intent' statements to yourself. And as you do this, remember that what counts is your inner experience. Furthermore, your inner experience will be amplified if you tune into your breathing and your heart, before you explore your feelings through saying the statements.

Let me offer you four general statements of intent that usually sum up our romantic yearnings. These are the four intentions that will enable you to succeed with this programme – notice now, without judging, if you already have your power of intent locked into these four statements, or if you need to perhaps reflect upon what it is you really intend to do here:

ONE: *'I intend to focus my attention regularly in the direction of someone new.'*

TWO: *'I am willing to spend time encouraging inner growth and healing.'*

THREE: *'I am ready to let go of old attitudes that stand between me and new love.'*

FOUR: *'I want to tap my deeper powers to actively attract love into my life.'*

I hope you feel free to change any of the words you might want to, so that you make these Intent statements your own. And please return to them a number of times during the next days, repeating them in whichever order comes most easily to you, so that you imprint upon your mind and soul your heart's intent.

There's a great power found in saying certain sentences that reflect the direction you want to aim your life towards. For years now my colleagues and I have been experimenting with what we call 'focus phrases' – clear positive statements that carry a special psychological and even spiritual power to elicit a strong inner response. Such sentences have the capacity to reverberate throughout the various dimensions of your mind and soul, stimulating associations, memories, ideas and feelings that in turn, provoke deep growth, healing and awakening. And repeating the statements will serve to further elicit new experiences which take you even deeper.

So I encourage you to return to these first four statements I've just introduced you to – and every day at least once for the next week or two, see if you can carry as your initial intent in this programme, the act of turning to the following page each time you return to the book – and move through the formal process where you say these focus phrases to yourself.

Exercise One: STATING YOUR INTENT

First of all, gently point your mind's attention towards the sensation of the air flowing in and out your nose . . . now expand your awareness to include the movements in your chest and belly as you breathe . . . and expand your awareness to also include the feelings you find in your heart, right in the middle of your breathing . . .

. . . and now, in this expanded state of awareness, go ahead and read each of the Intent statements to yourself – and in between each, pause for a breath or two or three, to reflect upon how you feel in saying this statement of intent – and then go on to the next one:

'I want to tap my deeper powers to actively attract love into my life.'

'I am willing to spend time encouraging inner growth and healing.'

'I am ready to let go of old attitudes that stand between me and new love.'

'I intend to focus my attention regularly in the direction of someone new.'

pause . . . experience

Chapter 2

Forgive and Heal Your Romantic Past

HEART ENCOUNTER – TWO

Zack was enjoying five days down in the Bahamas as a bonus his boss had given him for finally rising to the challenge, taking charge and scoring a large negotiation with his first major account. All Zack wanted to do was to sprawl out in the February sun and enjoy his perfect moment of hard-earned peace and relaxation. Life was good, he was feeling entirely satisfied with his own company. This was not a trip intended for any shallow romance, this was a recharge break and he was enjoying his own good company. He was not only feeling content with his business life, he was finally recovered from his last relationship and not feeling needy at all. On his second day of vacation he came in from the beach and showered, then headed down for lunch – and here's what happened:

> The elevator door was almost closed when I saw somebody hurrying to catch it. I kept the door open and a young couple got in. They were arguing and the man was obviously in an aggressive mood. The woman was calm in the face of her partner's arguing – and twice she looked directly into my eyes, as if asking me to forgive her friend's obnoxious behaviour.
>
> I was struck by the woman's eyes. She likewise the second time she glanced at me, got stuck in a gaze that was still going on when the elevator door opened. As the three of us stepped out of the elevator the woman's partner shouted quite loud at her, and then stomped off alone, leaving her standing there staring after him.
>
> As I observed the exchange, I felt a most curious sensation in my heart. I had determined that I'd stay out of any serious relationship for at least a year or so, and enjoy my success at work. But suddenly I realized that this woman was unquestionably special – and when she slowly turned her eyes away from her departing friend, and looked deeply into my own, I thought I actually felt her presence inside my heart as well as outside.

'Well,' she said, 'I guess I didn't handle that very well, did I. Jeff is usually not so bothersome. But I had to be honest, even if it hurt.'

I had no words to say. We stood just looking at each other, into each other . . . until I popped out of my spell. 'Well,' I said, feeling awkward but at the same time suddenly entirely calm and confident in this woman's presence, 'if he's not taking you to lunch, would it be entirely inappropriate for me to offer?'

'I – well, this is strange,' she said, seeming confused, and for the first time blushing slightly with a flush of emotion.

'You – I, we, well...' I blundered on.

Then she smiled, and her face softly lit up as if she seemed to recognize me. 'Who are you?' she said very quietly. 'What's going on here?'

I felt a surge of inner certainty from out of nowhere. 'I'm Zack,' I said. 'And hopefully I'm being blessed with your presence, who knows for how long.'

She continued looking into my eyes – then something inside her relaxed, she shook her head and laughed a beautiful light lilting laugh.

'What's so funny?' I asked.

'This, us – me,' she managed to say. 'And yes, please. Take me to lunch. I've been in a hell hole with that man for months now. He wouldn't let go. But just now – something changed.'

'I hope for the better,' I said.

'Oh,' she said, 'I can already tell – much for the better.'

We went together into the dining room of the hotel . . . and we've been together ever since.

B ecause they were both mostly healed from old emotional wounds, with hearts ready and open for new love, Zack and the new woman in his life were able to suddenly come face to face and recognize each other as kindred spirits. I shared with you in the Introduction my own experience of finally learning to heal my heart from old emotional wounds, so that I was ready for love in the present moment. If you're still caught in old heartaches and emotional confusions that keep you from being open to love in the here and now, I'd like to teach you my basic emotional healing and recovery process in this chapter, so that you can focus your attention directly towards times and people in your past where you got hurt deeply emotionally – and then forgive and let go of those times and people.

The stark reality is that you cannot love a new person while your heart is still wallowing in pain and resentment, guilt and denial about an earlier love affair. As long as you're stuck in the past, you can't love in the present – that's just how the heart works. So it's absolutely essential in this programme to take the time to forgive and transcend old lovers who still have a hold on your heart. The process isn't difficult once understood clearly, and it's such a massive relief to finally free your heart from past wounds and apprehensions.

In the process of this liberation process, you'll also find that you become more and more your own best friend. In fact in this chapter I'm going to help you explore the psychological fact that if you don't first love yourself just as you are, you really aren't ready for a successful relationship. The magic of lasting romance happens only between two people who have first of all resolved their past heartaches, and reached that point where they are quite content alone – then and only then can they come together and establish a relationship that is emotionally bright, anxiety-free and long-lasting.

Almost no one grows up without experiencing at least a few heartbreaks along the path to maturity. We don't often marry our first adolescent love. Rather we come together with youthful passion with someone – only to have that deep-touching heart bond get mercilessly broken. And by the time we're in our twenties, we've had our hearts broken at even more aching levels of suffering.

When we fall in love, and then have that love come to an end, it's very much like loving someone and then having them actually die – they are no longer in our lives, and we experience the trauma of loss that's emotionally very similar to grieving over the loss through death, of a loved one. The symptoms of grieving are the same, and the healing process the same also. The beauty of the human psyche is that it naturally knows how to move through a grieving process that heals the wound of loss of a loved one. The sad thing about the human psyche is that it often fails to move through this natural healing process – leaving the person stuck indefinitely in unresolved heart wounds that fester and pollute all attempts to establish new relationships.

If you feel you've fully recovered from past emotional wounds, feel free to skip fairly quickly through this present discussion. But if you still feel wounded in your heart by love from the past, please make this section especially important to you, as you move towards a new relationship. So many people jump from one relationship to the next without healing in between – and then wonder why the new relationship didn't work. The answer almost always is that the heart was unprepared for new love, because old wounds blocked deep heart bonding. Let's take care of that problem right now, so that your new lover doesn't have to get hit with negative emotions and inhibitions from the past.

No More Co-Dependence Please

Much has been said about the negative relationship condition called co-dependence. The condition is rampant in existing relationships everywhere, and certainly needs to be dealt with as a primary emotional health hazard. Here's how a co-dependent relationship happens. Two people who don't love themselves, who have a negative self-image and are the opposite of their own best friend, come together and give each other the love and acceptance that they cannot give themselves. They therein become dependent on the other person for their basic sense of self-worth, and their sense of being loving and loved. In essence they become addicted to each other for their daily hit of love and acceptance, and even if they aren't compatible and are failing otherwise in their relationship, they remain locked together in a co-dependent relationship that drags both of them down, and pollutes the lives of their friends and children as well.

Traditionally romance has been portrayed as a co-dependent relationship where you just can't live without the other person. You fully give your heart to this person, you give up your basic emotional centre – and then feel like you're going to die if you lose this person's love and attention. It doesn't take much work to unearth the roots of this type of relationship – it's what we had with our mother. But whereas with our mother when we were infants, it was true in essence that we were dependent on this person, as adults we're supposed to mature to where we stand on our own two feet emotionally, and are not needy like we were as infants.

Romantic love has a lot to do with infantile feelings when it comes to sexual relating, this is true – and it's wonderful. But I'm here to actively discourage you from becoming emotionally dependent on your new lover, because that is not the path to the deeper qualities of lasting love. Just the opposite – only when two people retain their sense of independent integrity and self-love can they plunge all the way into romance. As long as there's that lingering insidious infantile fear of losing the loved one and therefore ceasing to exist, there won't be the freedom and power and maturity to surrender to adult love.

Often when I talk about this element of mature relating, people react by thinking I'm asking them to give up what they consider the most satisfying aspect of a relationship – that of finally finding someone to take care of them, to cherish them and assure them that forevermore, they will be loved and nurtured and free from the fear of loneliness. Isn't that why we seek out a lover in the first place, to escape from the terrible feelings of being alone and unloved?

Relationships can be based on one of two primal emotions – love or fear. Co-dependent relationships are based on the fear of being alone. Independent relationships are based on a love that is not afraid of being alone. And I'm sure you can already guess that this issue all comes down to your relationship with your own self when you are alone. If you have low self-worth, if you don't really love your own self, then yes, you're going to hunger for someone to come and make you feel that you're okay, through giving you their love and acceptance – but you're going to lose your own centre in the process.

Likewise if you don't really love yourself, you're going to suffer especially terribly when a lover leaves you. Festering heartbreaks that just don't heal emotionally are almost always caught up in this deeper syndrome of chronically failing to love your own self. The overlong ache of heartache is really all about the devastating feeling that you have given your love centre to another person, and that person still has your love centre – so therefore you can't feel good about yourself without that person coming back to you.

I don't mean in any way to make light of this terrible situation because I've been there myself and know just how bad it feels. My point as a therapist is that if you want to finally break free from the ache of past relationships, the only healthy way to break free once and for all is to stop looking to other people for your ultimate inner sense of self-worth and lovability – and find your root grounding within your own independent heart.

Pause a few moments now, and take time to reflect upon how you yourself feel about what we've been discussing. Especially in things of the heart, never take the opinion of someone else as valid until you compare it to your own life, and what you know to be true. Tune into your breathing, and your heart's feelings – and explore for yourself: Does the above discussion ring true for you? Is your heart contracted in pain and fear, or open in love and hope? And are you seeking someone else to make you feel whole, or are you ready to feel whole within your own heart, so that the new love you yearn for can be free from co-dependence, and genuinely blossom?

pause ... breathe ... reflect ... experience

What Is This Thing Called Love

We now venture into one of the deepest topics there is. The topic is human love, and the power of this love in our lives. For me, love is not an idea. Love is not a philosophical concept. Love is an energy and presence in the world that underlies our entire existence. In the Bible you find the statement, 'God is love.' I consider that statement the most powerful expression of the infinite vastness and importance of love in our lives. In Buddhist, Islamic, Taoist and Hindu teachings the same basic realization is stated over and over – the power that we call our Creator manifests in the world through the energy we call love.

Romantic love deserves the highest respect in this regard, because the drastic power that draws two people together in romantic love ends up in sexual union which leads two people to the point of creating new life on this planet. The passion of sexual attraction is the movement of the Creator in our own bodies, leading to the spark of new life itself. And then when a new being is created, it's the radical power of motherly and fatherly love that nurtures that new being, creating the most powerful bond of the human heart, that of family. It's all of a whole – we come into this world through the spark of love between our parents, we live immersed in this love in our family, and then we become possessed by the power of romantic passion as young adults, and through the magic of this passion, are brought together into a new love union that creates new life.

Of course, often the act of physical creation of a new being isn't the aim or intent of a romantic union. I remember being in love and making love and feeling that in the act of making love, we were creating something even when pregnancy wasn't our intent. When we make love, we bring more love into the world through our hearts – and that's an act of ultimate creation as well.

A most curious thing about love is that we can't store it. We can't bring it into our hearts, and possess it. Love flows freely, it comes and goes – love is here purely to share, don't you agree? When we're 'in love' we're sharing that inflow of love through our bodies – and that flow of love through our hearts is surely one of the main things we yearn to experience.

Jesus and Buddha and other great spiritual teachers also talked about the dynamics of the inflow of love, teaching that we can only love others to the extent that we first love ourselves. Jesus said it like this: 'Love your neighbour as you love yourself.' In this love commandment he didn't expect human beings to be able to love their neighbour more than they love themselves – he challenged us to love others with the same love that we feel for our own selves.

Here's the psychological fact of love – you can only truly love other people when you have learned to love yourself first. Yes, you can become an addict to another person's affection and acceptance in a co-dependent relationship. But true love represents the flowing of the love you first feel for your own self, out into the world. Do you agree with this observation? My intent here isn't to tell you what to believe about true love, but rather to share with you my experiences, so that you can look at your own inner life and see what rings true for you. Our challenge is to look at the reality of love as it manifests in our lives, and learn how to live more and more within the flow of that love.

And so we come to the crux of the matter – how can we learn to love ourselves more, so that we have an abundance of love to give to those around us, and to our new lover in particular? Before I talk about my understanding of this question, pause a few moments now, tune into your breathing and the feelings in your heart, and see what insights you might have about how you can come to love yourself more deeply . . . where does love come from . . . do you have to judge yourself and shut out love . . . are you ready to let go of attitudes and assumptions that keep the infinite supply of love from flowing into your heart, and out to those around you . . . right here right now, are you wanting to let your old wounds heal, so that you can open up to love . . .

pause . . . breathe . . . reflect . . . experience

Becoming Your Own Best Friend

How do you in fact feel about your own self? Are you your own best friend? Or failing to be your own best friend, are you trying to find someone out there, to be your best friend? What are the qualities of a best friend anyway, and why do we all hunger for that special relationship, in or out of a sexual involvement?

Someone is our best friend when they love us just as we are. Best friends don't say we have to change in order for them to love us – they accept us one hundred per cent as is. This is the pure unconditional love that we hunger for. This is the true love that makes us feel whole, that enables us to relax and feel that we're okay. And perhaps more than anything else, we do hunger for the feeling of being okay, just as we are – because we know that deep down we don't really change that much. What you see is what you get.

The love of a best friend is a love without judgment. This love doesn't hold back anything. It's total, absolute, unconditional, one hundred per cent acceptant. And within the aura of such a love, we flourish. When we're accepted just as we are, our hearts shine and open, our creative energies surge, and our lives seem transformed for the better. This unconditional love is of course a primary aspect of romantic involvement. That's why we crave it so much, along with the sexual passion of course. We hunger to be accepted – first by our parents, then by our peers, then by our lover. And sometimes it seems we'll do almost anything to get that acceptance.

What I'm suggesting is that rather than trying to squeeze that acceptance and unconditional love out of someone else's heart, why not just give it to yourself instead? If you're really going to love your neighbour, or your lover, unconditionally, you're in fact going to have to learn how to love yourself first. And it's not that hard to do – in fact, the more I look at this act of self love, the more I realize what a tragedy it is that we don't teach children in school the ABCs of self-love. Yes, we teach a bit of self-esteem, but how about getting right down to the nitty-gritty of being our own best friend?

And here we come to the theme of mind management, because self-love and being your own best friend are a function of the thoughts you run through your mind, the attitudes you hold in the deep recesses of your brain, and the emotions that are stimulated by the thoughts you let dominate your mind. If you developed in childhood (from the attitudes of your parents and teachers etc) the underlying assumption that you're no good, that you're ugly, that you're unlovable, then your adult life is going to be polluted by these erroneous judgments – until you learn to identify them, and let go of them in favour of more positive self-assumptions.

Actually performing this mental shift towards more helpful attitudes isn't really so hard to do. What's seems hard is the initial realization that you have the power to make this shift. Old childhood programmings continue to dominate our lives only for as long as we let them. So I'm suggesting here that you begin to bring to light any negative attitudes about your own self, so that you can move through the natural process of discarding old attitudes that knock you down, as you embrace new attitudes that raise you up.

And here's the trick to all this, that does make it relatively easy to accomplish. Except in extreme cases where some cognitive therapy might be required, most of us do have the inherent power to choose new ways of feeling about ourselves – and that power comes from one simple ability that's crucial to a good life. We have the ability to simply decide that we're going to accept ourselves, just as we are. Period. We don't have to play years of mind games trying to replace negative with positive thoughts and images. All we need to do is advance a step deeper into our own psyches, and instead of holding the primary attitude that we don't love ourselves just as we are – just go ahead and take the leap. Over and over, consciously say, 'I accept myself, just as I am.'

The joke is, you've always had this freedom to accept yourself just as you are, to love yourself unconditionally. Acceptance and love are almost identical – they're the feeling that comes into our hearts when we stop judging. You can't really love when you're in judgment mode. Indeed, at any given moment you're either in judgment mode, or acceptance/love mode. And because you are the master of your mind, you can manage your mind so that most of the time, you're in acceptance/love mode, rather than in judgment mode.

Does this make sense to you? I know that for some of you, what I'm talking about here is new, and even a bit threatening. Many people think the world requires that we constantly judge, that we don't accept ourselves just as we are. After all, what would be the motivation for change, for improvement, if we loved ourselves just as we are? Well, curiously, deep change in our hearts and minds and souls happens only when love is present, wouldn't you agree? Love is the ultimate healer. I mean, if God is love, we're bringing God into our lives when we accept ourselves just as we are. And when we're judging ourselves, we're shutting God and love out of our lives. The older I get, the more this realization strikes me as a primal factor in human fulfilment or the lack thereof.

So let's shift from discussing the issue of love and being your own best friend, to exploring how you actually feel in your heart towards your own self. Please hold in mind that throughout this book, we're exploring who you are and how you feel not in a judgmental way, but purely to see the reality of the situation, and through observing the reality, encourage that healing and growth, that love and acceptance flourish.

After tuning into your breathing . . . your heart . . . your whole body here in the present moment . . . reflect upon how you feel towards each of the following sentences. Do this in a light-hearted mood, just playing with the statements to see all the different attitudes and judgments you might be carrying about yourself – which you can let go of in the process of accepting yourself, just as you are:

'I love myself, just as I am.'

'I don't like how I look.'

'I'm not smart enough.'

'I'm no good.'

'I feel really good in my heart about who I am.'

'Who could love somebody like me?'

'I'm hopeless.'

'I'm afraid to love again.'

'I'm okay, just as I am right now.'

If you feel that you already accept and love yourself just as you are, wonderful. If not, please begin over the next days to reflect upon the specific reasons you don't accept yourself just as you are. Here are a few questions to contemplate. You might want to get out pen and paper and write down answers to the questions, or reflect deeply upon them one at a time until you see your inner judgmental mind at work:

Question 1: What negative self-judgments are you holding in your mind that keep you from being able to love yourself?

Question 2: What are you habitually demanding that you change in your life, in order for your judging mind to finally accept you as okay?

Question 3: What would happen in your life if you decided to accept yourself just as you are, regardless of your weaknesses and problems?

Question 4: How would your life change if you opened your heart to your own self unconditionally, and became your own best friend?

pause . . . breathe . . . reflect . . . experience

Where Love Comes From

Romance and sexual fulfilment and the entire mating process is centred around this quality or power (or as some would say, this illusion) of love. Let's look a step deeper into your own beliefs and attitudes about love, so that you can consciously evaluate your existing assumptions about this power in your life, and advance those assumptions if they're outmoded.

What do we know about love, that we can all agree on? Well first of all, love is definitely an emotion that we feel in our hearts. The neurophysiologists tell us that the feeling of love is initiated by certain thoughts and associations in our minds related to early childhood experiences with our mother or another loving figure. When we perceive that someone cares for us and will protect us in one way or another, and that someone accepts us as we are and includes us in a feeling of family togetherness, then particular hormones are secreted in the brain and other organs of the body, eliciting physiological changes throughout our body, and especially in our heart muscles.

The feeling of love in our hearts is definitely not just a thought, it's a shift in the muscular and hormonal posture in our hearts that, in essence, feels good and further reminds us of early childhood experiences of being totally cared for and protected, accepted and cherished. This is the scientific view of love for most people – the materialist concept of what makes us feel good in our hearts.

Beyond this, new research is showing that the heart certainly runs on electrical impulses that are quite strong and scientifically detectable.

The heart generates a large electromagnetic forcefield that radiates outward into our environment, just as our bodies as a whole radiate a forcefield, and our planet likewise. I'm sure you've seen those drawings depicting the electromagnetic forcefield of the planet. Sensitive equipment has now documented the same type of 'torus' forcefield emanating from the human heart. This forcefield extends out at least fifteen feet on current measuring equipment, and therefore obviously reaches out and can be felt by other people near us.

The electromagnetic force-field of your heart broadcasts outward an energetic expression of how you're feeling in your heart – the forcefield changes its configuration considerably depending on what emotion you're feeling in your heart. So if you're feeling love in your heart, people around you are going to be bathed in this particular energetic expression of your feeling – they're going to 'pick up' your feeling of love, and literally be touched by it. So scientifically, love is definitely something you broadcast outward, and that you can receive as an energetic broadcast from another person if you're tuned in and sensitive to this broadcast.

Science has recently taken this understanding of love another step, in the Princeton Engineering Anomaly Study, which, over twenty years, documented that our hearts and minds broadcast an energetic power outward into the environment that can demonstrably influence the performance of very sensitive electronic equipment. The study also documented that our thoughts can influence the thoughts of a person we are focusing upon, and who is consciously receptive to our broadcast. Furthermore, this broadcast's power does not diminish with distance. Einstein predicted exactly this discovery of the power of human consciousness and intent in his writings. The intent of the experimenter does in proven fact influence the outcome of an experiment – and in extension, as we'll see, our projection of love out into the world is received by like-minded people wherever they might be.

Curiously, in the quite extensive Princeton Studies (I have this research posted at www.johnselby.com if you want to read through it) the researchers found that if they used lovers rather than solitary individuals for the 'intent experiments' their results increased not double as expected, but were six times stronger. Somehow the sexual love factor was a demonstrable factor in the research, indicating that when we're in love, our joined inner power to manifest is much stronger than when two strangers work on a project together.

So love even at scientific levels is not only an inner feeling, it's a demonstrable force that reaches out and affects the world, in still mysterious but definite ways. When we talk about the power of love, we're talking about real power. And this is a power that each of us can choose to increase within our hearts and minds and souls, and broadcast outward to make contact with potential lovers – even before we're physically close.

Spiritual Love

Science only takes us so far in understanding the deeper nature of romantic love. All cultures throughout the world carry deep traditions related to a quality of love that thusfar has proven too subtle to be detected on dials in experiments, but which is directly experienced in the hearts of almost all human beings on the planet. For lack of a better word, this quality of love is usually referred to as spiritual love – where the source of love is experienced as originating beyond our individual biological bodies. I'm not asking you to believe that this dimension of love exists if your philosophy of life is purely materialistic, but I do want to talk about how most people experience love beyond the strictly scientific model, because this experience plays deeply into our success in finding true love.

Whether or not it's a universal inner fantasy, or a universal spiritual reality, in all traditions we find the belief, based on general experience in the community, that the love we feel in our hearts flows into our hearts from a greater non-physical source, often called God. God's love is what drives every religion on the planet. And our openness to receive this transcendent power and quality of love into our lives lies at the heart of our success in feeling loved, and being a loving human being capable of lasting platonic, romantic and family love.

My experience as a therapist has been that a person's basic stance related to the inflow of love into his or her heart, determines pretty much everything else in that person's inner life, romantic and otherwise, including self-esteem and personal happiness. Furthermore, each of us has the power to choose to open our hearts more to love. We directly control the inflow of love into our lives – if we only realize we have this control.

In my secular meditation book *Seven Masters, One Path*, I teach a basic approach to opening our hearts to this inflow of love from beyond our individual ego centre. Whether this process is based on a scientific metaphor or a spiritual truth doesn't really matter in terms of its effect. And in fact, I suspect that scientific metaphor and spiritual truth are one and the same thing. The experience we all know is that when our hearts are shut to love, no love flows in. And when we open our hearts to love, a most beautiful inflow of love is experienced.

When you are your own best friend, one of the main choices and acts you make each new day is to regularly take time to consciously open your heart to the inflow of love. Rather than waiting passively for some other person to come along and aim their love into your heart to make you feel loved, you have the power to bring love into your own heart on your own. And as we saw before, to avoid co-dependent relationships it's essential that you be the one to initiate this inflow of love into your heart and life. It's vital that you become your own best friend and take responsibility for regularly opening your own heart to receive love – and not from just one person, but from the infinite supply of love that does seem to emanate from God or the Creator or whatever theological name you give to that Ultimate Source of Love that permeates the universe.

Being your own best friend means feeling love in your heart for your own self. And where is that love going to come from? In my experience, that love comes from the inflow of infinite love. And what enables that love to flow into your heart? Your own decision to put aside thoughts that you're unlovable – and to open your heart to the inflow of love. It's that simple, even though it's infinitely sublime at the same time.

If you want to be a loving person who will attract a like-minded loving person, then your responsibility is to first bring love into your own heart, so that you have love to share. Be your own best friend. Accept yourself just as you are – and through this process of accepting yourself just as you are, open your heart to let love flow in and fill your heart.

Let me share with you the basic focus phrases that will enable you to regularly turn your attention in this vital direction of loving yourself and opening your heart to the inflow of love. If you pause a number of times each day, tune into your breathing and your heart, and then say these sentences to yourself and open to a new experience, you will activate your own step-by-step process of becoming more loving, as the love flows in more and more:

Choose to take a bit of time to nurture your own inner love for yourself . . . turn your attention to your breathing . . . the air rushing in and out your nose right now . . . the movements in your chest and belly as you breathe . . . your heart, right in the middle of your breathing. And say to yourself as you exhale, 'I accept myself, just as I am . . .' Allow these words to reverberate throughout your being, encouraging you at least for the next few moments to go ahead and love yourself just as you are. You can then say, 'I love myself just as I am . . .' and experience as these words encourage the experience they're pointing your attention towards.

And when you're ready, say to yourself, 'My heart is open to receive the inflow of love . . .' and allow yourself to feel your heart opening up, and love flowing in. Choose to let the love flow in, and experience for yourself what happens as you continue breathing. Be open to a new experience each time!

pause . . . breathe . . . reflect . . . experience

Forgiving Yourself First

We started this chapter talking about how important it is to recover from old heart aches and to forgive the transgressions of our former lovers, so that we can heal our hearts and be ready for a bright new love. Then we seemed to get distracted by the idea of, first of all, becoming our own best friends. The reason I've spent so much time exploring the power of becoming your own best friend is that you can't really forgive your old lovers and recover from the wounds of your romantic past, unless you've first of all forgiven and made peace with your own self. So let's go the final step in this self-love process, and then apply what we've learned to forgiving and making peace with old lovers. You'll be surprised at how easy it becomes to forgive old lovers, once you've done the same process with your own self.

The universal inner process of forgiveness is one that many people have difficulty even approaching, let alone moving through. Especially when it comes to forgiving one's own self for things done or left undone in the past, we have a really hard time transcending the emotion of guilt and shame, and healing our hearts from our self-inflicted wounds of guilt and shame.

Do you carry feelings of guilt and shame towards your own self, for things done or left undone in your past? If so, these feelings will directly thwart your ability to love yourself just as you are, and open your heart to the inflow of love. If you feel you've done bad things that make you unworthy of being loved, even by yourself, then this primal negative judgment against yourself will short-circuit your hopes of romantic love because you're denying love to your own self, and that makes you basically unlovable by other people.

Pause for a few moments, reflect upon whether you continue to judge yourself as bad, sinful, unworthy and unlovable, because of things you did in the past. What do you need to forgive yourself for doing in life? What keeps you from being able to love yourself just as you are? Why don't you allow love to flow into your heart?

pause . . . breathe . . . reflect . . . experience

Forgiving And Healing

How can you take your life in your own hands, manage your mind to your advantage, and break beyond the prison of guilt and shame? How can you forgive yourself for what you've done in the past, so that you can love yourself in the present moment? From a psychological point of view, there's a most liberating answer to this primal life question. Psychologically, forgiveness and acceptance are basically one and the same. Forgiveness is always aimed at an event that happened in the past. We forgive ourselves for what happened in the past, to the extent that we simply accept that this event did happen – and in the act of accepting the past, we set ourselves free from it. This acceptance can be stated clearly: 'Yes, I did that deed, or failed to do that deed, in the past. And because I cannot change the past, I accept that reality fully.'

The primary fact about the past is that it is over and gone – and therefore you can't ever change it. So many people fight against what happened in the past. They refuse to accept that an event happened – and thus stay hung up on that event. But here's our saving grace – as soon as we stop fighting the reality of the past, and accept fully in our hearts that something did happen, something remarkable happens in our hearts and minds. As we surrender and accept what happened in the past, we let go of that event. It is gone, it's over. You can't change the past – but you can let go of it, and return your heart's valuable attention to the present moment.

When you say to yourself, 'I did such and such in the past, but I can't accept that I did it because it was wrong,' you generate guilt and shame, and remain stuck in the past and your judgment of the past as somehow bad or wrong. Forgiving yourself means finally saying, 'Okay, I did that. It's over. I'll try to do better. And I fully forgive myself for doing it.'

This is such a simple act, yet most people go through their whole lives holding onto certain past events without forgiving and forgetting. The result is that we perpetuate negative emotions and self-images – we feel that we're bad people who don't deserve to be loved. Are you caught in this guilt-shame syndrome that keeps you from being your own best friend?

Religions often help out in this situation by pointing out that God is all-loving, and that God's love can heal the past, bringing forgiveness that wipes away all our transgressions. This universal religious belief points towards the basic psychological process we were talking about earlier – the conscious step of opening our hearts to a love beyond our individual creation, that comes flowing in when we make the choice to let it flow in.

I'm not here to preach any particular religious belief. What I've found is that psychologically, regardless of our religious or secular philosophy of life, we ourselves must make the conscious step of forgiving ourselves for deeds of the past, and we must also open our hearts to let healing love flow in to empower our act of self-love. My experience of emotional healing in general is that it happens when we finally choose to accept the past, and then take the next essential step of consciously opening our hearts to the inflow of love. And as this love comes flowing into our hearts, it completes the healing process – and sets us free of the past, so we can fully love in the present moment.

Most therapists and ministers agree that this process of accepting the past, and then opening to healing love, is the most direct and powerful way to forgive and move on in life. How can we best tap this process in our everyday lives, so that we can forgive ourselves, forgive our former lovers, and heal?

The answer lies in taking a few minutes one or more times a day to pause and say carefully chosen focus phrases that point your mind's attention towards the process, and thus encourage your heart to open up and experience the healing process. The core success of this book rests on your taking this time regularly, to encourage the growth and insights you need, in order to prepare yourself for a true fulfilling heart encounter.

Let me walk you through this basic daily process that will hopefully become a healing routine in your life from here on out. Of course the first few times you try this process, you're still in the learning phase and not much might happen. Please trust me here – I'm giving you the essence of many years of therapy work and experience. This process can rapidly transform your life, by helping you manage your mind and awaken your soul in directions that enhance your heart's potential to love and be loved.

As always, begin by turning your attention to your breathing experience . . . and the feelings in your heart right now as you breathe . . . be open to a new experience . . . accept whatever feelings you find . . . and on your next exhale, say to yourself: '*I accept myself, just as I am* . . .' Breathe into the experience these words stimulate.

And say to yourself, '*I forgive myself, and let go of the past.*' Breathe into whatever experience comes to you this time, through the power of these words.

And now say to yourself, '*Right now, my heart is open to receive healing love.*'

Breathe into whatever experience comes to you . . . be open to a new experience . . . let your heart open, let the love flow in.

pause . . . breathe . . . reflect . . . experience

Recovering From Heartbreak

Learning to let go, to accept and forgive and become free from the past, does take time. What's important is that each new day you do take time to encourage the process of emotional healing – if you don't act, there's no one else who's going to. What I'm offering you are specific actions that you yourself can be sure to make each day, so that rather than feeling stuck in loneliness and guilt and anger and hopelessness and all the other emotions that so often accompany a heartbreak and solitary times, you can go into action regularly to improve your condition and prepare yourself for the love you yearn for.

You've just learned a beginning process to help you forgive your own self, and in the process become your own best friend. Let's move on to see how you can apply this same basic process to forgiving former lovers, as you learn to accept what happened, and encourage a flow of love that will heal the past – so that you become free to live and love again in the present moment.

Again, you'll find that the way you manage your mind will dictate your success in transcending old heartaches and moving on. For instance, many people hold on to the belief that their old lover somehow wronged them, hurt them, and continues to be responsible for the inner emotional torments related to the breakup of a relationship. Blame is in fact a central focus in the hearts of people who can't let go and recover from a former affair. But is such blaming of another person for our present emotional aches really valid?

I've observed that as long as you're caught in the habit of blaming someone else for your own present-moment emotions, you remain unable to change those emotions in positive directions. When you blame others for how you feel, you make yourself a victim and lose your power to take charge of your own feelings. Do you tend to do this?

The reality of emotions is that they are a response to the thoughts you continue to think and the related images and memories that your thoughts stimulate. And in psychological fact, you yourself are responsible for the thoughts you think. If you continue to turn your mind's focus of attention back to when your lover left you or did something that caused you emotional trauma, you are the one responsible if those memories continue to provoke renewed anguish. Your former lover isn't running your mind right now, you are. And if you begin to realize this, and to assume more and more conscious control of where you focus your moment-to-moment attention, you'll discover that indeed, you can choose not to focus on that episode of your past. In any given moment, you can focus your attention where you want to – hopefully in directions that make you feel good, not bad.

So if you find that you're regularly holding in your mind thoughts about how someone else is to blame for how you're feeling right now, begin to realize that you are the one who's managing your mind so that it thinks thoughts that provoke emotions that make you suffer. As long as you believe and think to yourself, 'Such and such was mean to me and broke my heart and is responsible for me feeling bad right now,' sure enough, that's going to be the reality you live in. But you do have the power to say to yourself, 'I'm in charge of my feelings, I can focus my attention in directions that make me feel bad, or in directions that make me feel good – and I'm going to choose to feel good!'

This basic realization that no one else is making you feel bad can transform your life. As soon as you stop blaming other people, and assume responsibility for your own feelings, you become empowered to manage your mind so that most of the time you're feeling good – and this is a major life victory! You have shifted from victim to victor. Are you ready to make this shift?

Every time you find yourself feeling bad, look to see what thought you are thinking, that is stimulating that bad feeling. And if you find that that thought causes you pain, then you can choose to stop fixating on that thought. That's mind management at its best. At any given moment, you can choose to think about a million different things. You can remember the most terrible event in your past, and run that memory through your mind over and over, and make yourself feel absolutely terrible. Or you can choose to remember a wonderful experience, and feel wonderful. That's your power!

As you'll find throughout this book, my primary suggestion is that as much as possible, you choose not to drift off into the past at all. Why? Because it's over and gone. Going into the past isn't going to satisfy your yearnings to meet someone and get on with your romantic life. The present moment, rather than the past, is going to be your best friend in succeeding in your desires, because all of your life actually emerges right in the present moment – this is where yearnings are fulfilled, not then. And each moment, you have the choice of sinking into memories and reflections upon the past, or holding your attention here in your body in the present moment – where literally, it's all happening.

So the primary recovery from heartbreak is actually a recovery of the present moment. All heartaches are caused by dwelling on the past. If you want to break free from the agony of heartbreak, you must begin to reclaim the present moment as the primary place you hold your attention. We're going to spend the entire next chapter focusing on how to do just that.

But before you make the step of choosing to live more in the present moment, it is important to state clearly your intent of letting go of the past – and in order to let go of the past, it's essential to accept what happened to you in your previous relationships, and to forgive the people who you've been blaming for your heartbreak. To stop blaming those who broke your heart is to become free in your heart. And you can do this quite simply, if you'll just devote a few minutes each day for as long as it takes to fully accept, forgive and let go.

Here's the basic action process, based on what you've learned earlier, for forgiving and moving on. You say certain focus phrases that stimulate an inner action in the direction you want to move. Each time you say the sentences, you'll open yourself to a new experience that will encourage further healing. And as the days go by, you'll find your heart healing, the past less important, and your present-moment life expanding.

Let's walk through this for the first time, so you can begin to learn the process and repeat it each day until you're free. I'll guide you through the full process you've been learning in this chapter. As mentioned earlier, if you want further guidance in doing this session, you can go online to www.johnselby.com and listen to my voice guiding you through the process, or you can order the audio CD and listen to the session through your stereo system.

Exercise Two: EMOTIONAL HEALING

Set aside a few minutes, and make yourself comfortable however you want. As always, begin by turning your attention to your breathing experience . . . the air flowing in and out your nose . . . the movements in your chest and belly as you breathe . . . and the feelings in your heart right now . . . be open to a new experience . . . And accept whatever feelings you find . . .

On your next exhale, say to yourself: *'I accept myself, just as I am...'* Breathe into whatever experience these words stimulate. Perhaps say the sentence again, as you stay aware of the changing feelings inside you.

And now say to yourself, *'I forgive myself, and let go of the past.'* Breathe into whatever experience comes, through the power of these words. Let go of judging yourself and enjoy the expansive feeling in your breathing, when you let go of guilty feelings, and love yourself without reservation.

And now say to yourself, *'Right now, my heart is open to receive healing love.'* Breathe into whatever experience comes to you . . . be open to a new experience . . . let your heart open, let the love flow in.

Now allow the name and face of a former lover to come to your mind, someone you still feel bad towards, or blame for your broken heart. In your imagination, meet this person's eyes honestly, and say to them, *'I forgive you for what happened, I let go of all bad feelings, and accept the past.'* Allow this feeling of acceptance to fill your heart . . . let it all go.

Now again turn your full attention to your breathing . . . let your breathing stop when it wants to . . . and start again when it wants to . . . and expand your awareness to also include your heart, right in the middle of your breathing . . . and say to yourself, *'My heart is open to receive . . . healing and love . . .'*

And with every new breath, let love flow into your heart, into your whole body, as you enjoy the wonderful feeling of love permeating your entire being . . .

pause . . . breathe . . . reflect . . . experience

Chapter 3

Wake Up Your Sexual Presence

HEART ENCOUNTER – THREE

Natalie's husband had died two years before and, being a bit over fifty with grown children and loads of good friends, she wasn't expecting true love to grab her again this lifetime, even though she was often lonely at night. She'd had such a wonderful marriage for nearly thirty years – who could replace that man? On Christmas Eve she bundled up and went next door for a block party, feeling quite content with herself, and anticipating the fun next day with her grandchildren. She walked into the party, got a drink – and here's what she experienced:

> I wasn't feeling all that social and didn't see anyone to talk with, so I went into the library room and picked up The New Yorker. I could hear laughter from the other rooms, but I felt very good just relaxing alone.
>
> I noticed someone walk into the room and looked up – it was the fellow who lived around the block from me, Hans something from Europe. We knew each other a bit, being from the same neighbourhood. He nodded to me, said something friendly, I don't remember what – and then walked over and stood by the window, staring out at snow falling in the porchlight.
>
> I read a couple more New Yorker jokes, then found myself stretching and yawning, feeling very good in my body. I looked over to where Hans was standing. He was looking right at me intently. But it wasn't the Hans I knew casually – I was looking deeply for the first time into the eyes of the most beautiful soul, whose expression seemed on fire with the same feeling that suddenly struck me. There was an almost electric charge that snapped between our bodies. I felt like I was fifteen as a sudden sexual passion took hold of me. He came over and sat down on the sofa – I could hardly breathe. And as if it was the most natural thing in the world, without even thinking I reached and took his hand – and without words, he leaned towards me and we kissed – and a crazy dam of long-blocked lust broke inside

me. There was no stopping that kiss. Our host came in and found us making out and she was shocked for a moment — but then we were all three of us laughing. As she closed the door to give us our privacy, the most exciting romantic explosion you could imagine continued deep into the night — and even better yet, it's still going on.

N ow that we've spent necessary time exploring how negative memories of the past can drag you down into perpetual heartache, it's time to explore how proper focusing on the present moment can raise you up towards the most beautiful new times of your life. Specifically we're going to discuss ways in which you can manage your mind so as to bring more pleasure and passion into your body, and in the process generate an attractive aura around you that people will respond to positively.

Your ability to open up and enjoy simple physical pleasure, and allow unbridled sexual energy to come flowing through your body, will prove central to success in any realm of romance. If you want to be desirable as a sexual partner, it's essential to learn how to allow good feelings to take over your entire being, so that passion – and ultimately orgasm and total consummation in sexual fires – is something you not only desire, but regularly experience.

How can you learn to regularly increase the pleasure potential of your body? How can you become genuinely more sexy and desirable, so that you do attract a desirable mate into your bed and heart? To answer this question we'll need to look directly to your own sexual feelings, inhibitions, yearnings and behaviour habits, to help you prepare yourself for your new lover. I hope you feel comfortable as we speak frankly about the more intimate aspects of your own sexuality. This is not an erotic sex-manual by any means – but we do require a fully honest exploration of what romantic love is all about, and how you can surrender to your own sexual passion without any lingering inhibitions to thwart your otherwise-positive sexual future.

Let's first of all talk about pleasure in general, and especially how your past conditioning has influenced your relationship with feeling good inside your own skin. You came into this world with a remarkably sensual, even erotic body. The simple touch of your momma's finger on your tummy could set you off laughing in a most lascivious way. As an infant you almost certainly possessed all the natural human capacities for experiencing great sensual delight through all the various mediums of infantile stimulation and pleasure. And without doing anything in particular, you spontaneously enjoyed the various sensations of each and every new moment that came to you, unless a moment arose when you encountered direct pain, hunger, cold or the panic of possible danger.

Babies are so full of pleasure and joy because they live entirely in the present moment – they aren't thinking about any problems at work, they aren't worrying about something they said to someone yesterday, they don't drift off at all into memories of the past or dreams of the future. Babies are very much present-moment creatures, and likewise, pleasure itself is entirely a present-moment affair. Our bodies by definition don't experience sensory pleasure in the past or the future – right here and now in the sense organs of our bodies and the pleasure centre in the brain and the host of hormonal secretions throughout the body is where the actual experience of pleasure happens.

Therefore one of the first laws of pleasure is that you need to regularly master the fine art of returning your mind's focus of attention back to the here and now, if you want to enjoy feeling good in your body. This is a primary act in mind management – that of consciously reclaiming the present moment. Almost everything you'll be learning in this book later on will be based on your growing ability to say, 'Hey – I want to take charge of where I'm focusing my power of attention, and I want to focus it where I find pleasure in life.' This act is a clear act of self-love – choosing to manage your mind so that you maximize good feelings. You're being your own best friend by choosing to focus your attention where you find pleasure – and pleasure is found right here, right now, in what we call the eternal unfolding of the present moment.

The act of returning your attention regularly to the present moment also brings you into the exact coordinates where sooner or later you're going to encounter your new love. The present moment is the only place you will find your new lover because all experience happens in the here and now, not the there and then, right? So learning to focus experientially on the here and now is vital for succeeding in the romantic hunt and coming face to face, in the present moment, with the person you're seeking. And once you encounter your new lover, your ability to tune into pleasure and to fully enjoy all the various ways in which you and your lover can share pleasure will determine much of what develops in that relationship. After all, who wants a lover who can't put all else aside and tune into his or her body? How much more crucial can things get?

But the reality is, a great many people have great difficulty doing just that – for a host of reasons we don't even need to get into here, most of us have inhibitions and aversions and just plain self-defeating mental habits that make us shy away from tuning into pleasure. I'm here to help you get over these outdated conditionings, as you prepare yourself for the optimum love that's on its way to you.

I've already taught you the basic mind-management technique for shifting into the present moment. Let's now expand this process specifically towards discovering and nurturing good feelings in the body. The most direct path to the present moment from the point of view of both the world meditation tradition and cognitive psychology is to first of all choose to take conscious control of your mind's focus of attention, and then to aim your power of attention to the most active ongoing present-moment happening in your body, which is your own breathing experience. Right – the air flowing in and out your nose right now.

Have you stayed aware of this most intimate and obvious sensory phenomenon while reading deeper into this book, or did your breathing somehow disappear along the way somewhere? No problem – we just keep returning to the sensation of the air flowing in and out your nose as you read this (and mine too as I write) and allow that sensation to pop you back here into the present moment. You know that you're alive because of that sensation in your nose. And if you're aware of the pace and power of your breathing, you're tuned into your emotions at the most direct level.

And here we go with the second expansion, where you actually expand your mind's awareness to include two sensory happenings at the same time – the sensation of the air flowing in and out your nose, and at the same time the sensation of the movements in your chest and belly as you breathe . . . and pow! By tuning into two or more bodily sensations at the same time, you shift your mind's awareness into an entirely different realm of consciousness than its usual two-dimensions cognitive-thinking function. Notice for yourself how when you become aware of your nose and your chest and belly at the same time, something almost magical happens – you shift from two-dimensional mental reality to three-dimensional physical reality.

Thinking is a two-dimensional flat experience. Your thoughts don't have volume after all. But as soon as you become aware of all the different sensations coming to your awareness as you breathe, you tune into the dimension of volume in your body, and it is in this dimension that all pleasure is to be found – and you just found it.

Practice makes perfect, and that's what I'm here to help you with. So follow my words, and observe your inner experience expanding as you turn your mind's attention to the air flowing in and out your nose right now . . . let your breathing come and go on its own . . . make no effort. Just pay attention to the sensations as they come to you. You never breathe the same breath twice, they're always new . . .

And now as you stay aware of your nose sensations, allow your attention to expand to include the sensations in your chest and belly as you bring air into your lungs, and then blow that air out

. . . all those various sensations happening at the same time! And you can practise this exercise to where you can experience all of them at once. That's what consciousness expansion is all about, right there. And you can do it, right now . . .

pause . . . breathe . . . reflect . . . experience

How Your Heart Feels

Love of course is all about your heart. I know that many of you are aching in your hearts right now, suffering genuinely from the chronic lack of a shared heart experience. And when you're hurting in your heart, all too often the tendency is to try to avoid feeling that inner pain altogether. So many people respond to the ache of loneliness, abandonment and romantic despair by going mostly numb in the heart, and holding their focus of attention anywhere else but – in the heart.

I ask you to trust me when I say, if you want to find true love, no matter how bad your heart hurts right now, we need to gently turn your attention more and more towards your heart – because only through shining your loving attention right where it hurts can the power of your loving attention help to heal the old emotional wounds of the heart, so that your heart can, indeed, love again. I know this will at first be difficult for some of you, but I also know that if you'll allow me to show you this basic healing path for an aching heart, you'll be so glad you did!

Let's continue with our refresher course on expanding your awareness – to include your heart right in the middle of your breathing experience. While aware of the air flowing in and out your nose . . . and at the same time the movement sensations in your chest and belly as you breathe . . . expand your awareness another notch to also include the feelings in your heart, right in the middle of your breathing . . .

Every time you do this seemingly simple meditation, you're going to have a new experience in your heart, and of your heart. You can never really predict what you're going to find in your heart, each new time you look. The trick is to look without judgment, so that you can feel directly the truth your heart is feeling right at that moment. I mentioned that we need to accept the past because it's already happened and we can't change it. The same is actually true of the present moment we just tuned into. In the act of turning our focus of attention to our feelings in the present moment, that particular present moment instantly turned into the past too – and so whatever feeling you find when you look to your heart, simply exists. You can't change what you just felt. All you can do is acknowledge the feeling.

But here's the amazing thing – as you continue to observe the feelings in your heart, the power and content of your own attention is going to begin to interact with your feelings, and those feelings in your heart are going to change! If you look to the feelings in your heart, find them painful or frightened, and judge them negatively, rejecting them as feelings you don't want to focus on at all - your power of attention will serve as a strong negative force that further pushes your heart feelings in painful rejected directions. There's no worse feeling than being judged by some powerful presence as somehow bad, and rejected.

However (and now you'll see why being your own best friend is so important) if you gently bring your attention to the feelings in your heart, and whatever those feelings are, accept them with loving attention, then something positive will happen to the feelings in your heart! The power of love that you're beaming upon your heart's feelings actually has the power to heal those feelings, to soothe them, and transform them. Even though science has yet to find a way to document this phenomenon with dials and meters, we all know that compassionate love heals our emotional wounds. What I'm showing you is how you can take responsibility for healing your own heart wounds, through the power of your own non-judging attention.

And the bottom line here is this – if you don't heal your own heart and bring good feelings into your body as preparation for a significant romantic encounter, don't be surprised if the person you are attracted to is NOT attracted to you, because you haven't done your homework. Instead, you're liable to find yourself, as mentioned before, getting involved with someone who likewise is packing a wounded heart – and your relationship will be built upon co-dependent dynamics of soothing each other's wounds, rather than the pleasure that comes when such wounds are already healed.

So let me guide you with words that point your mind's attention towards your heart. First of all tune into your breathing . . . the air flowing in and out your nose . . . the movements in your chest and belly as you breathe . . . and now expand your awareness to simply observe and experience whatever feelings you have in your heart right now . . . don't in any way judge what you find . . . accept yourself as OK just as you are, even if you're hurting or afraid in your heart . . . just continue to breathe . . . and allow your loving attention to shine upon your heart feelings . . . and with every new breath, be open to a new experience as your heart feelings respond to your loving attention, and begin to soften . . . to become trusting . . . and open up to receive love . . . allow healing to take place . . . enjoy!

pause . . . breathe . . . reflect . . . experience

The Giant Pleasure Organ

It's all about tuning into our breathing, and our heart. It's also all about turning our mind's attention towards that largest organ of our body which is so very much fixated upon giving us pleasure – or yes, pain upon occasion. I'm talking of course about the essential sensory/sensual organ that covers your entire body with its vast network of remarkably sensitive nerve endings – the skin. Even your direct sexual organ – penis or clitoris – is covered in this amazingly sensitive covering.

The skin is almost always underrated as an organ. The truth is, the skin is the largest organ by weight, even bigger than the heart and the brain. Not only that, like the heart, more than fifty per cent of the skin is made up of nerve cells identical to those found in the brain. Who knows what levels of intelligence are reached by the organ called our skin – but certainly our experience of sensual pleasure is an all-body experience orchestrated by billions upon billions of dedicated nerve endings that form a phenomenally complex neurological presence.

And once again, just for the record – these sensitive nerves don't stimulate you with pleasure happening in the past or the future. Pleasure coming from the skin is a pure present-moment experience. So as you learn to quiet your past and future-fixated thoughts, and tune more intensely into the present-moment sensations being gathered by the entire outer covering of your body, you awaken to a most remarkable potential for pleasure, be it the pure sensory pleasure of a breeze blowing against your cheek, the overall sensation of feeling good inside your own skin – or the radical sexual pleasure of a lover kissing and caressing your naked body in the heat of passion.

There's one other dimension to feeling good in your body that I want to include here – the nerves throughout your muscular system that also report back to the brain. Working in harmony with your skin perception, these interior nerves give you a feeling of the position you're holding with your whole body, and also respond to hormonal changes which indicate if you're basically feeling tense and bad in your body, or relaxed and good.

When you put all this together, you have the almost infinitely intricate neurological system that generates the experience you feel in any given moment, of your whole-body presence and pleasure. When you're lost in thought or memory or imagination, you lose this whole-body sense of presence and pleasure. Only when you choose to turn your focus of attention to your present-moment experience do you come alive again in your body.

My recommendation for the rest of your life is that you develop the new mental habit of maintaining some of your mind's awareness on your present-moment whole-body experience, no matter what else you're doing. Yes, often you'll still drift entirely away from your body as you get lost in thought. That's fine. But as much as possible, if you want to live a life that feels good, and that keeps your body charged with positive radiance, you're going to want to make whole-body awareness a key signature of who you are.

This focus on positive body awareness is how to stay sexy – because sexy people are exactly those who are attuned to the pleasure they're feeling in their physical bodies every moment. What a difference it makes to people looking your way when you walk down the street, for instance, if you're lost in thought and not present in your body, or mostly focused on the sensory pleasure of walking. And certainly in bed with your lover, the ability to stay mostly in your body rather than in your head is vital to a good sexual experience.

You are one fantastic pleasure machine – but only if you choose to be one. Let me show you what I consider to be the fastest and most powerful way to make the choice to be a sensual creature, each and every moment of your life. Again, we're building here on what you've learned already, so that the learning process remains relatively simple to accomplish:

As you read these words, or any time you want to bring your awareness back to your whole-body presence and pleasure, choose first of all to turn your attention to your breathing . . . become deeply aware of being a living creature who's naturally breathing in and breathing out . . . enjoy the expansion and contraction feelings . . . and now expand to include the feelings in your heart, accepting whatever you discover in your heart . . . open up to the inflow of love and good feelings in your heart . . . and now move right on into the final expansion, as your experience expands to include your skin's entire surface area at once . . . so that you're aware of your whole body as a living three-dimensional whole, here in this present moment . . .

pause . . . breathe . . . reflect . . . experience

Pleasure Hunt

At first this expansion of your awareness to include your whole body at once might seem difficult to attain, but all it takes is a little practice. This whole-body awareness is after all what you felt as an infant almost all of the time – before you got older and started thinking and thus drifting off into the past and the future. All I'm suggesting is that you return to a quality of awareness that was your constant companion when you were very young – so it's not at all difficult to do. Your challenge is just to remember to do it, and to take the time to bring sensory pleasure into your life.

Right now, for instance, consider your posture as you read this book. Are you holding yourself in a tense or uncomfortable position, even while reading about being nice to yourself and bringing more pleasure into your life? Or are you letting your body find a comfortable position as you read? Notice that even as you continue reading these words, you can also tune into your body and the relative sense of pleasure or lack thereof that you find. And notice that as soon as you give yourself per-mission to feel good in your body while reading these words, things start to happen – you naturally move a bit, perhaps stretch, discover some good feelings somewhere – and assume a more comfortable position while reading.

When I moved to Hawaii and had the chance of setting up my living and writing space however I wanted, I purposely put my writing office about a three-minute walk from the house, so that every time I wanted to take a break from writing and business, to go get a drink or a snack or chat with my wife or take a short nap or whatever, I could enjoy a short walk from office to house and back again – because like everyone else, movement is the best way to make my body feel better.

And while I was over at the house stirring some soup on the stove just now, I noticed our cat in the living room lying in a shaft of sunlight, since it's cool today. The cat noticed me come into the room, and responded first by standing up and stretching that long languorous cat stretch that epitomizes good feelings in the body. For a moment I stood reflecting on how almost all animals in the world take time regularly to stretch, to relax, to enjoy the present moment. And during those moments I was lost in reflection, I was mostly gone from my own body – lost in thought. Then I popped out of the thought, and joined my cat, doing some simple yoga stretches myself.

And even while I'm sitting here typing away at my computer, imagining you sitting there reading these words, and feeling our sense of connection through these words and feelings, I also maintain an awareness of my body sitting here – and allow my feet to move as they want to, stretching sometimes. Often I stretch, and sigh, and otherwise keep my whole body happy while I sit here typing. And I encourage you to do the same on your side of this communication link – while you read, also be aware of your body, and give it permission to move as it wants to, and assume positions that feel good.

It seems that at any given moment, no matter what we do, there are a few places that don't feel especially good in our body, and a few places that feel downright wonderful – and a lot of places in between that aren't really drawing our attention one way or the other. If we habitually look to see the negative in life, of course we're going to fixate on the pain and aches and uncomfortable feelings that are reaching our brains from sensations originating in our skin and muscle nerves. Here again we see the almighty power of choice regarding where we're going to aim our mind's focus of attention. Because we can also choose to focus where there's pleasure happening in our body, moment to moment.

Right now, there are almost surely a bunch of good feelings here and there in your body, going to waste because you're not being your own best friend and pausing to enjoy these good feelings. Imagine going through a whole life and very seldom pausing to enjoy the pleasure that lives in your body. What a terrible waste of pleasure, and what a mean thing to do to yourself – ignoring what makes you feel good!

Let me share with you a basic sensual exercise you can do almost anywhere, to practise focusing on good feelings inside your body, so that you more and more reap the present-moment harvest of your own inherent pleasure:

After reading this paragraph, I encourage you to put the book aside for a few moments (or longer if you want) and get comfortable either sitting or lying down. Tune into your breathing . . . your heart . . . your whole body here in this present moment . . . and with your eyes closed, begin to allow your mind's awareness to move over your body, looking for good feelings. And when you find good feelings, focus there for a while, enjoying the pure pleasure of your body . . . and then move on looking for other places in your body where right now, there's a good feeling just waiting for your attention!

pause . . . breathe . . . reflect . . . experience

Choosing To Feel Good

As you prepare yourself for what you hope is going to be that primary love encounter of your life, let me ask you this question: are you hoping to team up and be totally intimate with someone who doesn't feel good inside their own skin? Are you looking for a lover who doesn't know how to shift into pleasure and surrender to sensory bliss? Are you hungry to be in bed with someone who fixates on pain and thus grumps around in a bad mood because life sucks?

Well obviously, no. You don't want a lover who's out of touch with the vast realms of pleasure in the body. You want a lover who delights in the softest touch, who gravitates towards pleasure, who luxuriates in the pure glory of good feelings everywhere, and we do mean everywhere, in the exotic temple of life we call the body.

Now we simply turn this around. Is the person you seek in life going to want a partner who's caught up in every little ache and pain of the body, and meanwhile ignoring the good feelings happening at the same time? Is this love of your life going to want a lover who hasn't done his or her erotic homework and learned new positive habits of erogenous delight? In a word, have you prepared yourself sensually, to match the lover you seek? Or are you like so many unsuccessful romantics who expect their lover to somehow miraculously make them feel good all the time?

I hope you begin to see just how important the preparation stage of this game is, for long-term success and fulfilment in the mating game. If you look back on relationships in your past that just didn't somehow work, I'm sure you'll begin to realize that one or both of you almost certainly were making choices, out of habit, that sabotaged that relationship. Not having learned that you can manage your mind to you and your lover's benefit, you perhaps didn't focus much at all on feeling good inside your own skin so that you brought to your lover a presence that was bright, positive, overflowing with good feelings.

Please don't feel guilty if this is so. As we've seen, guilt is a total throwaway emotion that gets us nowhere except depressed. Instead, you can accept how you were, readily forgive yourself for not having known how to manage your mind and emotions better – and now in this present moment, even as you read these words, realize that you can choose right now and forevermore to encourage good feelings in your body. You can choose to enjoy the feelings in your breathing, for instance. Each new breath brings you life – what joy! And because movement in general feels good, you can relish the sensations of movement in each new inhale and exhale.

It's all in how you choose to see life. You can choose to go around with the attitude that life is a drag – and sure enough, it will be. You can fixate on all the failures in your life, all the bad things you've done, all the worthwhile things you left undone – and definitely, you're going to feel like hell, and project that feeling out to people you meet. And you can blame everyone around you for your problems, grump about what a sorry state the world is in, lambast your boss for being such a meanie – and sure enough, the world's going to punch right back at you.

Conversely, what's really keeping you from just saying, 'Hey, given the choice, I choose to focus on the good rather than the bad, the pleasure rather than the pain, the love rather than the hate, the hope rather than the despair.' And sure enough, you'll begin to fill your mind and your life with goodness, pleasure, love and hope. Your choice – each and every moment. With each thought you let run through your mind, you're choosing your destiny. Realizing this, the notion of mind management so as to choose the destiny you want becomes vital.

I have listened to clients, when faced with this primal notion of choosing to feel good rather than bad, as they reel off one 'but' after another, listing all the reasons they have that support their negative attitudes of why life has to be suffering and pain, difficulty and despair. Yes, there are very logical attitudes and beliefs in every culture for why we should choose to feel bad. And if you want to continue to buy into those beliefs and attitudes, that's your choice. All I'm saying is that there is an alternate choice – and that choice is always awaiting your go-ahead.

From now on, see if you can watch the thoughts that run through your mind. Notice if the thought makes you feel good, or makes you feel bad. And when you see a thought go through your mind that makes you feel bad, realize that you don't have to think that thought. Right at that moment, you could turn your focus of attention elsewhere to where you find good feelings, hopeful thoughts, and positive outcomes. Even if you're in a room full of people fixating on their anger, their anxiety, their hopelessness and despair, you have the freedom to find some little place in your body that feels good – and hold your focus of attention there so that good feelings begin to increase within you. And sure enough, you'll begin to radiate good feelings, and there will be at least one beacon of love and peace and pleasure in the room.

And the good news is, that love and peace and pleasure will spread – it just takes one person to risk choosing to feel good, and everyone around them can feel this radiance from that person's heart, and feel a touch of good feelings in their hearts as well. That's our hope in this world. Tend our own garden, heal our own hearts – and let the love flow into our bodies. That's our primary responsibility, as I see it. Choose to prepare our hearts so that they receive loads of love on a regular basis – and then broadcast that love out into the world. Not only will we find the true love we yearn for romantically when we do this, we'll touch other hearts and wake up their love potential as well.

Perhaps you're old enough to remember the traditional song: 'Everybody loves a lover, I'm a lover, and everybody loves me, yes they do – and I love everybody since I fell in love with, fell in love with, fell in love with you!' My simple suggestion is that we fall in love with our own selves first, so that even in our preparation stages, the love comes flowing in, and spreads . . . That's our choice!

> Pause a moment if you want, and reflect upon your own preference for pain, or pleasure. What are your habits – do you focus on the negative, or the positive? And are you your own body's best friend? Do you love yourself? And if not, do you want to? Are you ready to change your choices, so that you encourage good feelings and a good life?

pause . . . breathe . . . reflect . . . experience

Waking Up Your Sexual Presence

At some point in the next days or weeks, you're going to once again venture out into the world seeking true love. And naturally one of the primary questions you'll be asking yourself is whether you are attractive enough to draw to you someone you'll be sexually and energetically satisfied with. To end this chapter, let's look deeply into your present sexual presence and attractiveness – and see where you might want to act, to wake up your sexual presence to higher levels of attractability.

As we discussed before, having a body that matches the present media concept of the ideal sexy figure is not what being attractive is all about. Certainly it helps if God granted you a perfect figure, and also if you keep in shape so that your physical appearance is optimum. But the power of attraction between two bodies is based on something far deeper – which of course explains why people of all body shapes end up finding true love, and also why people with perfect physical figures can end up alone and lonely.

I'm sure you've walked down the street and seen someone who was not necessarily handsome or beautiful by media standards, but who still struck you as really quite attractive anyway. Why? Because this person was feeling good inside her or his own skin. When we feel ugly or depressed or angry emotionally, we definitely project an unattractive presence in the world. And as we've seen, when we're full of joy, acceptance, love and brightness, we project an attractive energy into the world.

There's also another dimension to this question of being handsome or pretty or just outright sexy – and that's your basic energy level, or what's referred to as your energetic body. Sexual presence definitely involves a particular charge of energy in the body – an energy that seems to possess a magnetic power to attract other people's attention. Scientists are presently struggling to understand the exact nature of our energetic body, but there's no doubt that we do have such a thing. And how we manage our energetic charge is as important as how we manage our thoughts and emotions – in fact at the core of our being, it's basically impossible to separate them all. They interact with each other intimately to produce what we call our sexual presence.

Being sexy is almost always equated with being charged with a particular quality of energy that touches other people both in the genitals, and hopefully also in the heart. Sexual presence definitely has to do with an inner feeling that is broadcast outward and received by other people. Your own sexual presence can be seen in how you walk, how you smile, your tone of voice, your posture, your physical readiness for action. But what's driving all this – what's the power behind your sexual presence?

I've been exploring this question for years now, and I've found several different ways to talk about this most mysterious quality that drives all of romance. Certainly your natural sexual endowments play a part in your attractiveness – but I've worked with absolutely beautiful movie stars who were utter failures when it came to romance off the movie set, and known physically quite ugly people who possessed a remarkable positive sexual charge and presence.

Sexual presence is more an inner emanation of a feeling, a self-image, an energy – and a particular powerful intent. Let's look at each of these in turn:

SEXY FEELINGS: The inner feeling that generates and radiates a strong sexual presence, as we've seen, is that which emerges when you regularly choose pleasure and are tuned into good feelings in your body. A sexy person is clearly someone who already is in touch with his or her erogenous zones – who radiates the promise of great sex in the future by already being plugged into his or her sexual feelings in the present moment. And please note that sexual feelings aren't just felt in the genitals. As we'll explore later, the entire body is one great erogenous zone, and a sexy person is someone who is feeling good as a whole-body sensation. Especially when heart and genitals learn to function as one greater powerhouse, sexy feelings become very deep, and carry the power to manifest your deeper intent.

SEXY SELF-IMAGE: If you see yourself as unattractive and ugly in your mind's eye, that's what you're going to radiate, even if you have a beautiful physical body. When your self-image is negative, your entire sexual presence is short-circuited. Conversely, regardless of your physical prowess, if your self-image embraces yourself as a sexually awake and eager person, your sexual presence will be strong. And again, it's your choice ultimately, regarding how you're going to see yourself. You can re-create your self-image by choosing to feel good in your body, and letting that good feeling transform your sense of who you are. And once again, when you learn to integrate mind, heart and genitals into one loving presence, your self-image becomes whole, and radiates strongly.

SEXUAL ENERGY: In later chapters we're going to plunge right to the heart of your energetic body and see where this energy comes from, and how you can increase it. For now, our point is that if you pull the energetic plug on your sexuality, there's nothing there at all. Ultimately, sexual energy is the power of the universe flowing through your individual body, pushing for sexual union and the creation of a new being to help continue our species upon this earth. Our survival as a species depends on the flowing of sexual energy in our bodies, bringing us together to reproduce and keep the human dance going – so of course, the inner power and sexual push that moves us into action is vital to sexual presence and fulfilment. A third time, let me mention that sexual energy is not just a genital phenomenon – only when head, heart and genitals come together as one greater energy field does your energetic body radiate the deeper attraction that will bring a like-minded person into your arms.

SEXUAL INTENT: A great many lonely people with otherwise ready systems for romance flounder right here. They might have great bodies, a positive sexy self-image, and loads of sexual energy driving them – but in their minds they don't admit honestly their primal romantic intent. In many ways, intent is all-important in life, and nowhere more important than in succeeding in romance. When you see someone who's real sexy walking down the street or at a party or at work, what you're seeing is someone who is willing to let the world see his or her yearnings, hungers, desires – and intent. When you are ready to let the world, or at least certain people, see into your heart and perceive your intent to fulfil yourself sexually, then all other internal systems fire off beautifully and you become energetically attractive, and at some point successful in your heart hunt.

Let's see how you presently rate yourself on these four scales of readiness for successful romance. Please hold in mind that this entire book is focused on helping you to attain readiness with these four dimensions of sexual presence and romantic empowerment. As you read the questions, pause and tune into your breathing with each, and let insights come to you – don't judge yourself, just be honest:

Sexy Feelings: Do you often feel sexy in your whole body, especially when you're moving (walking, dancing, running, stretching etc)? Or is this an area where you want to focus as you prepare yourself for your new lover?

Sexy Self-Image: Do you usually see yourself in your mind's eye as sexy and attractive to those around you, projecting a presence that is openly sexual and ready for love? Or is this a dimension that you want to explore in more depth, and transform to your advantage?

Sexual Energy: Are you usually filled with good sexy energy as you go about your day, with plenty of energy free for sexual attraction? Or do you want to learn how to enhance your general charge of sexual energy, so that you radiate an attractive force-field that will bring love to you?

Sexual Intent: In your own heart, and in your relating with others, are you already clear and honest about your intent of wanting to actively fulfil yourself sexually and at deep heart levels? Or are you now wanting to learn how to clarify and express your romantic intent?

pause . . . breathe . . . reflect . . . experience

Exercise Three: SEXUAL AWAKENING

At the end of each of these beginning chapters I'm introducing to you a certain component of the daily programme you'll want to do during the next days and weeks, to prepare yourself for new love. In the first chapter, I introduced the basic process of stating your intent, so that your whole being regularly expresses your intent to fulfil your romantic yearnings and find lasting love. To end the second chapter, we explored the basic daily process for encouraging emotional healing and recovery from past romantic wounds. Now to end this third chapter, let's move through the daily process for encouraging the awakening of your natural sexual presence.

The aim here, as in the earlier sessions, is to memorize specific focus phrases that carry the power to resonate throughout your mind and heart and body, pointing your attention in primal directions that we've identified as very important preparation areas for a fulfilling sexual relationship. Let me say again that each time you say one of these sentences to yourself, you'll have a new experience. My understanding of personal growth is that it's an incremental process – each moment, each new day, you're ready to have a particular new insight or experience, that deepens your sense of who you are, and what you want in life. Each time you say one of these focus phrases, your whole being will respond with the insights and feelings, realizations and awakenings you're ready for right then. And over days and weeks, you'll find that the pace of your awakening picks up considerably, as you surrender more and more to the natural healing and inner growth process we're nurturing through this programme.

So right now, as you're just learning the process, move fairly quickly through the whole process so that you get the feeling of what you're doing, and begin to memorize the key sentences. The beginning of mastering such a programme always focuses on learning the structure by heart, so that later on you can put aside the effort of remembering, and plunge directly into the awaiting experience that each focus phrase elicits. As mentioned before, if you want more specific audio help, feel free to join me at www.johnselby.com for audio guidance.

Make yourself comfortable . . . stretch if you want . . . yawn perhaps . . . tune into your breathing . . . let your breaths come and go on their own . . . and expand your awareness to include the feelings in your heart . . . accept the feelings . . . breathe into them . . . and expand your awareness another step to include your whole body at once, here in this present moment . . . and let your mind explore your whole body, and find places where you feel good . . . enjoy feeling good physically . . . stretch and move if you want to . . . give yourself permission to feel wonderful right now . . .

And now see what experiences and insights come, when you say to yourself:

'I give myself permission to feel good right now in my body.'

When you're ready, open to a new whole-body experience as you say to yourself:

'I feel sexually attractive and ready for love.'

And finally, say to yourself:

'My intent is to be sexually attractive and romantically fulfilled.'

And now you can just relax . . . let go of all thoughts . . . tune into how you feel in your body right now . . . give yourself full permission to feel good . . . stretch and move if you want, to increase good feelings . . . let your sexual energy flow throughout your body . . . and fully indulge in the pleasure of being a sexual being!

pause . . . breathe . . . reflect . . . experience

Chapter 4

Discover Your Heart's Attraction Potential

HEART ENCOUNTER – FOUR

Bernard had been doing the attraction meditation (see page 136) and all the rest for months and sometimes he felt discouraged because romantic lightning hadn't struck at all yet. But he was feeling more and more at home and even downright good otherwise in his life. There was loads of love coming to him in his meditations – and then one evening he felt it . . . the sense that yes, there was someone in particular out there, tuned into him heart to heart. And then –

I went to work the next morning almost expecting to run headlong into my one true love – but instead I had to sit through a seemingly uneventful meeting. My supervisor asked for someone to volunteer to catch a plane the next day and give a presentation to a new company on our list. I almost never do such things – but without even thinking, I found myself raising my hand. I just had the feeling that I wanted to say yes – and so I did.

That night I was doing my attraction meditation, and again the feeling came flooding over me that I wasn't alone, that someone was aware of me, and I could feel her presence. I'm not at all an esoteric person and the feeling was quite spooky to me – but also exciting. So off I went the next morning to a city I hardly knew at all, and before I knew it I was standing in front of about thirty people giving a presentation. About ten minutes into the presentation was when it happened – I glanced at the audience and caught the eye of a woman out there. She was staring intently at me, rather than half-bored like the others. And for a moment I even lost my train of thought and had to look at my notes to continue with the lecture.

She was wearing a blue sweater and, try as I might, I couldn't make my eyes stop returning to her, and my heart from pounding. Maybe she wasn't the most beautiful woman in the world, I'm not the most handsome man – but to me she was so sexy, it was all I could do to continue with the presentation.

And then I was surrounded by questions and had to go off to a luncheon with several of the top people in the company – and she was gone. My mood crashed, I was almost rude to my hosts. And flying back home on the plane that afternoon I felt so dejected, it was an agony. My mind started to plot ways that I could get a list of everyone at that meeting, so I could try to contact the woman in the blue sweater. I felt consumed by her presence, my heart was aching for her.

That night I had to force myself to sit down and do my attraction meditation – I was almost angry at the whole process because it had brought me almost within touching distance of my true love and then I'd lost her. For ten minutes I made myself turn my focus of attention to my breathing, my heart, my whole body in the present moment. Nothing. No feelings at all – just this aching. At some point I was so charged with agitation and confusion and all sorts of other vague emotions that I stood up, went over to my open window and shouted as loud as I could out at the farmland in the distance!

Then I calmed down, went back to do the meditation – and even before I could move my mind through the basic attraction process, suddenly there she was. I could see her face and feel her smile and I almost melted with emotions in my heart and a rising power in my genitals as well – I want you!

When the phone rang I must have jumped ten feet in the air. The bubble was popped, I had lost her again. I went a bit aggressively to the phone.

'Hi, what is it?' I said impatiently.

'Oh,' a woman's voice said. 'Is something wrong?'

'Oh, I don't know. Who is this?'

She was silent a moment. 'Who do you think I am?'

For just a second I had the sudden powerful desire that it was that woman in the blue sweater from the distant city – and like a fool I blurted out – 'Uhm, blue sweater?'

Again she was quiet a long moment. Then – 'I just had to call, I hope you don't mind.'

'It's really you?' I asked.

'Yes, it's really me.'

'Thank God,' I blurted out. 'I was afraid I'd lost you.'

I am certain that you have often felt your heart, and your whole body and soul, yearning intensely for new love. Your heart, as we've already mentioned, is in fact a quite large electromagnetic force-field, as is your whole body. And those intense feelings of yearning and desire that fill your heart and body aren't just romantic ideas or fanciful emotions – they're very real energetic emanations that reach out beyond your body and touch other hearts and souls.

These very same intense yearnings and all-powerful desires that make your heart ache with loneliness will also, when properly prepared and aimed, provide the positive energy to draw your new lover towards the desired encounter with you. So while you're mastering the process learned in the previous chapter of awakening your whole being to your own inherent sexual brightness and power, let's also now explore more deeply the more advanced process that will turn your romantic desires, yearnings and hungers into a magnificent radiant force that will reach out and bring love to you.

Yes, you can learn to enhance and direct outward into the world your own presence, qualities and intent, to attract like-minded lovers towards you. This is in fact, upon closer examination, exactly how successful relationships come into being. Let's get right down to the scientific and intuitive nitty-gritty of how your sexual passion attracts similar and resonant sexual passion. Hold in mind throughout that I'm not asking you to believe my understanding of this attraction power.

All I'm asking is that you explore with me what you yourself feel inside your own heart when you look right to the core of your yearnings. Discover for yourself the truth of your heart's power to attract a desired partner from a distance – that special person already waiting out there for you, who at the right time will be in perfect congruence as you awaken your heart's potential to reach out and make contact.

Your Whole-body Heart

To move further towards the actual reality of how your body works energetically, we need to purposefully expand our notion of what we mean when we talk about yearnings of the heart, or romantic desires and hungers. Love certainly has its centre in your heart in your chest, you know this without question. Romantic yearning is a function of the heart. But at the same time, romantic love wouldn't exist at all if that yearning wasn't also a function of your sexual centre in your body, down lower in your genitals. And right between the two of these, heart and genitals, there's a third centre of great importance in your body's energetic system – your power centre deep in your belly.

When you are caught up in yearnings for a fulfilling sexual relationship, all three of these energetic centres are actually working in union, each providing an essential element to the whole experience of romantic hunger and desire. There's also a fourth energetic centre in your body that actively experiences the feelings of desire – your throat and mouth. In this chapter I want to teach you how to integrate your feelings in each of these energy centres of the body, into a greater whole-body powerhouse that you can purify and direct at will, to achieve your desired goal.

I've found in my work over the years that most people who are struggling to find the right lover and life partner to share their lives with, have one or more of these four energetic centres mostly shut down, or overly active. You know for yourself that when you meet someone who is overly fixated on sex, for instance, but has his or her heart centre shut down, this person is hard to relate with and ultimately won't prove to be a true friend and mate. Likewise if your heart is aching wildly for love but you are denying your sexual passion, it's hard for romantic love to find you. And similarly if your power centre is turned off for one reason or another, you just don't have the oomph to get out and actively engage in a new relationship. And so many people have their vocal centre constricted to where they can't express their feelings, and engage in the oral dimensions that are so important in sexual love.

Elsewhere I've written whole books on the energy centres of the body, for those of you who want to explore this in serious depth. But rather than getting over-deep here in all sorts of scientific and esoteric discussions about the body's energy centres that provide the energy needed to become truly attractive in the deeper sense of that word, let's turn directly to your own experience for verification, and advancement. For our purposes here, you can fairly quickly come to understand and master the basic programme for activating your whole-body/heart potential.

First of all, once again, let's tune your attention into your own heart. Let me guide you through the basic process (practice makes perfect!) of tuning into your heart, and then we'll expand to also include the other whole-body/heart dimensions:

Even while reading these words, expand your awareness to include the sensation of the air flowing in and out your nose . . . expand your awareness another step to include the sensations of movement in your chest and belly as you breathe . . . and now expand your awareness another magnificent step to include whatever feelings you find in your heart right now . . . breathe into these feelings . . . accept them . . . allow them to change with each new breath as you accept how you feel in your heart . . . and let healing love flow into your heart . . .

pause . . . breathe . . . reflect . . . experience

Once you've made this primary heart contact, let's see what happens when you begin to tune into your specific heart yearnings for new love. You know this feeling very well, it's what promoted you to pick up this book in the first place – you have a hunger for fulfilment that is driving you forward towards your coming encounter and union with your new lover. Let's bring that yearning directly into focus now:

> As your breaths come and go, allow yourself to tune into your hunger to meet someone who really turns you on, who is strongly attracted to you, and who fulfils your dream of a satisfying sexual partner . . . let each new breath bring this almost aching hunger stronger into your heart, so that you surrender to the powerful inflow of desire to come together with your new love . . .

pause . . . breathe . . . reflect . . . experience

And now, let's explore what you actually feel energetically down in your genitals, when you are focused on your romantic yearnings and desires. Yes, I'm going to be quite frank here about your sexual energies. After all, this is a natural healthy wonderful dimension of who you are, and in the security of our discussion in this book, you can freely look in the direction of your sexual energies, and explore how to use this energy to help empower your romantic process.

As you read these words, allow your mind's awareness to expand to include not only your breathing experience and your heart feelings, but also your feelings down in your genital region. Do you feel alive down there, or is there somewhat of a disconnect between your heart and your genitals? Let's find out, and begin the evolution towards full integration of heart desires and sexual passion. Rather than just expecting the same old thing when you look to your genitals, please be open to a new experience as we do this – because it's the newness that makes sexual relating come alive, the willingness to put aside memories and expectations, and discover unique new feelings and powers that are coming to you in this utterly new present moment:

So stay tuned into your breathing experience, coming and going without any effort at all . . . expand to include the feelings of passion and desire in your heart right now . . . and expand your awareness again to include your sexual presence down in the genital region of your body . . . go ahead and move a bit if you want, to wake up this area . . . and as you continue to focus your attention on your yearning for sexual fulfilment, let yourself feel that yearning also down in your genitals . . . acknowledge that you are a sexual person, and yes, you have feelings down there that are powerful, and hunger for total fulfilment with a true love partner . . .

pause . . . breathe . . . reflect . . . experience

Now that you feel both your heart and your genitals together in their desire for sexual fulfilment, with the more romantic feelings of the heart mixing beautifully with the wild raw hungers of the genitals, let's expand another step to include the power centre of the body, that actually gets things you want done, done. There's no worse aching to be found in the human body than that heart-genitals ache when it has no action power to move it towards actual fulfilment. This is why at some point it's so important to check out your power centre in the middle of your belly, where your push and shove comes from to break beyond your habits of inertia, and get out to accomplish that which you yearn for so powerfully.

Again, tune into your breathing, which continues to pulsate with your basic life force . . . and expand to include your heart feelings, which hunger for true oneness with another wonderful human being . . . and now expand to include your genitals, where your heart's desires turn fiery in the anticipation of crazy sexual passion . . . and with heart and genitals both aching for action and release and fulfilment, expand your awareness to include your power centre in your belly, where your heart's yearnings and your genitals' hungers fire up your charge to go into action . . . feel a growing pressure in your belly to break beyond depression and hopelessness and all the rest, and start physically moving in the direction of your awaiting lover . . . breathe into this rising power . . . enjoy your discovery of rising energy that will carry you to your goal . . .

pause . . . breathe . . . reflect . . . experience

So now you have a beginning feel for how to consciously bring together often disparate energies in your body – heart, genitals and power centres. I find it essential to also include the throat/mouth/lips centre because so much of our hungering is felt here, and so much of our desired sexual expression and interaction happens in this centre as well. The human sexual response, after all, includes a most powerful hunger to sexually gobble up the love partner. Equally, the sounds we hunger to make during intercourse are obviously oral in nature, emerging surely from our sexual and power centres deep down in the body, then manifesting through vocalization.

One final oral point – studies in the Seventies and Eighties showed that much of the human sexual response is short-circuited if the jaw muscle stays tense and the teeth closed. Our biting reflex is in fact very important to our sexual expression – and we directly block our power when we block our biting reflex. This reflex is expressed in the oral act of dropping the jaw as we exhale through the mouth. Many people who are repressed sexually have this habit of blocking their biting reflex. This in turn turns off their basic power to get out and get what they want in life, including a lover.

If you have your biting reflex blocked, two things happen. First of all, you block your basic instinctual capacity to defend yourself if attacked, through biting. Of course we don't go around biting each other these days – but the primal bite-defence reflex remains hard-wired into our nervous systems. Many of us who, for one reason or another, have come to fear the unleashing of our own power, have developed the unconscious habit of keeping the teeth clenched and jaw muscles tight, as a perpetual guard against the expression of our own power. To consciously break this habit is to free up your belly power – and that's vital to getting what you want in life.

Also, when you're constricted in your throat and mouth, your verbal expression is obviously inhibited, which can cause problems both when you're initiating a relationship, and when you're becoming intimate – sex is all about oral interaction at intimate levels, as I'm sure you know. Orgasm comes when the jaw muscles are relaxed and mouth open – it's as basic as that.

So yes, over the next days and weeks, let's make sure to focus regularly on your oral power centre, and prepare you fully for heart encounter and erogenous fun. Here's the beginning process:

Again, tune into your breathing . . . let it come and go freely for a few breaths . . . and now expand your awareness to include your feelings in your heart . . . open up to all your romantic desires and passions that so often fill your heart . . . and also tune into your genitals . . . let yourself wake up down there – feel your rising power . . . and also tune into your power centre in your belly . . . feel your rising energy to go into action to satisfy your desires . . .

And now expand your awareness to include your tongue . . . your throat . . . your jaw muscles . . . and your lips . . . open your mouth and breathe freely through the mouth and see how this feels to you . . . bite a few times with your teeth to feel that biting reflex in action . . .

And now on your exhales, make a few growls . . . smile and growl at the same time, with your mouth wide open as if to bite! . . . and now say out loud (unless you're on the subway of course) – 'I'm hungry for love! . . . I'm hungry for love! . . . I'm hungry – for love!' . . .

And now just relax, breathe freely . . . notice how you feel in your heart . . . in your genitals . . . in your power centre . . . in your throat and mouth . . . and be open to a new integrated feeling of your power throughout your body . . .

pause . . . breathe . . . reflect . . . experience

Sexual Power and Pleasure

We are all born sexual animals. Not only should we readily admit this erogenous fact – we should shout to the high heavens our praises of our sexual nature. We're hard-wired to experience the most utterly exquisite wild crazy physical and emotional and spiritual pleasures with our sexual partner, in the act of intercourse or even just in the heat of a passionate glance. Even with all the religious and cultural inhibitions most of us were programmed with, most of us one way or another find expression of our sexual appetites on a regular basis – and hopefully fully enjoy that expression while it happens.

Obviously as you prepare yourself for what you hope will be that final lasting relationship you so hunger for, you're going to want to thoroughly check out your own sexual condition and upgrade to higher levels of potential pleasure and sexual sharing where you find remaining inhibitions and bothersome attitudes and programmings. Let's get blunt and to the point so we can rapidly evaluate your sexual readiness for a fulfilling erotic relationship. Good sex certainly isn't everything in a close relationship, but it's an integral part of the whole picture.

PAST LOVERS: When you look back and remember each lover you have had in your lifetime, what do you find? Did any of these lovers fully satisfy you at the time? Were you able to let go and entirely surrender to passion and orgasm – or have you had problems becoming uninhibited and sexually wild? And did your lovers find satisfaction with you, or for some reason were they not fulfilled? Take a few moments now to look back, remember . . . and let new insights come about you as a lover.

SELF-STIMULATION: Most of us masturbate when we don't have regular sex with a partner. Many people masturbate even when they have a good sexual partner. And it seems that everyone has sexual dreams, especially if they aren't making love or masturbating regularly. Yes, we do need to come, men and women alike. Our sexual pressures build up genitally, and demand release. There has been much unfortunate judgment against masturbation in most societies, but most people do it. In your case, do you still feel guilty when you masturbate? Have you become your own best friend sexually to where you enjoy stimulating yourself and bringing yourself to the point of coming? Take a few moments now to put the book aside, as you reflect upon your own masturbation habits and preferences – and if you accept your recurrent sexual charge that needs release, one way or another . . .

EROGENOUS ZONES: Each of us has our particular favourite ways of being sexually stimulated. What about you - do you admit to all your favourite pleasure zones, so that you can tell your lover what you like? Do you feel you've fully explored your own sexual preferences, and really know your erogenous zones fully, or are you still learning about yourself? For instance, are there just a few places and things that turn you on – or is your whole body an erogenous zone, so that your skin everywhere enjoys being touched and caressed? Pause a moment or two and remember experiences where one of your erogenous zones, head to toe, was exultant with pleasure . . . and openly say to yourself, yes, I like that, and that, and that . . . and I want to share that pleasure with someone!

SEXUAL PREFERENCES: Some people like to make love soft and quiet, some people prefer loud and wild. What sort of lover are you, and in what directions do you want to move in your sexual expression? This is important because getting clear on what kind of love you are hungering for will help you attract a similar lover to you. I don't care if you're straight or gay, wild or quiet, this or that – all I care about is whether you openly accept and embrace your own desires and hungers sexually, and are ready to be with someone who likes what you like, and wants to do what you want to do – get clear on this, and life unfolds beautifully. So pause and reflect upon what you like, what you want, and who you want to be with to do all that . . .

pause . . . breathe . . . reflect . . . experience

Choosing Your Charge

If you are going to actively attract the right person into your life, you're going to need a clear strong sustained charge of attraction energy in order to accomplish this goal. Let's get clear on what feelings in your various energy centres provide positive attraction energy, and what feelings in your energy centres reduce your power to attract. Once you begin to consciously take responsibility for managing the energetic charge in each of your four energy centres, your potential for attracting your lover into your arms becomes amplified greatly.

Let's quickly move through a list of feelings in the heart that will attract your lover, versus feelings that push a potential lover away from you. This list is very important to contemplate often in the next days and weeks, so that in the actual attraction meditation you'll be doing each day, you'll know what feelings to focus on:

Feelings That Attract	Feelings That Repel
Compassionate	Heartless
Joyful	Depressed
Loving	Hostile
Curious	Bored
Sensual	Irritated
Bright	Dull
Energetic	Lethargic
Optimistic	Pessimistic
Alert	Vague
Playful	Grumpy
Happy	Sad
Accepting	Judgmental
Courageous	Fearful
Friendly	Mean

Psychologically one of the truly remarkable things about how our minds and hearts and souls work, is that we can focus on a particular word that represents a particular feeling, and begin to feel that feeling just by saying the word to ourselves and opening to experiencing that feeling. We can nurture joy in our hearts simply by holding the word 'joy' in our minds and hearts as we breathe. Joy begins to grow inside us, when we focus on it – yes, we can nurture a special positive feeling simply by holding the word for that feeling in our minds and hearts. Talk about power!

But most of us tend to do just the opposite. We fixate on negative feelings and thoughts, and mull over upsetting memories and apprehensions. Even though we have the choice of feeling good or feeling bad based on what emotions we choose to focus on, all too often from past conditioning we choose the negative over the positive. For instance, do you ever sit around thinking to yourself, 'It's hopeless,' rather than holding hope in your heart? Do you find yourself grumbling with irritation or anger or judgmental feelings, just out of habit? Do you stay stuck on thoughts that blame other people for your problems, or that make you mad at others? Hey, we all do.

I want to offer you a daily programme that you can do, to consciously begin to shift your heart feelings from negative to positive – and why not? Given the choice, and also given your intent to attract someone positive into your life, this is the most direct route to awakening qualities in your own heart which will attract those qualities in another heart.

Right now, as you tune into your breathing . . . and your feelings in your heart . . . say to yourself the word, 'loving', and let yourself start to feel loving in your heart . . . say, 'I feel love in my heart' and open up to the inflow of love . . . say, 'I feel joy in my heart,' and let that feeling begin to expand within you . . . say to yourself, 'I feel sensual in my body,' and let good feelings spread . . . and say, 'I'm ready to love,' and let this feeling radiate out to the world around you . . .

pause . . . breathe . . . reflect . . . experience

Singles Blues

You have the power to choose what charge you're going to carry in your energetic system – a negative charge of emotions that will repel a lover, or a positive charge of emotions that will attract a lover. Please consider the section you just read as a primary focus for the next days and weeks, so that you actively manage your heart and mind in directions that will make you attractive.

Now we come to the equally vital question of whether your charge of attractive energy is high or low. If you feel hopeful that your lover is literally or figuratively just around the next corner, chances are you're going to be feeling a high charge of good feelings in your heart and other energetic centres in your body. If you have fallen into hopelessness and despair over ever finding your one true love, you're probably packing a very low energetic attraction charge. And curiously, if you have reached the point where you are no longer feeling emotionally needy, and have become your own best friend, your energetic charge is probably in optimum condition to attract your lover. Let's look further at these variables, and explore how you can consciously act to raise your charge of attraction energy.

Many single people first of all go around for a while with a high charge of rather needy energy as they struggle to find an idealized partner to make everything okay in their lives – but fail in this attempt because their emotions are both tumultuous, unrealistic and conflicting. Then when no ideal lover appears, they sink into low energetics as self-doubt, hopelessness, guilt, anxiety and other negative feelings pull them down into a painful lethargy and despair.

Then hopefully (with or without this book) they finally let go of seeking another person to make them happy, heal their own hearts and become satisfied within their own skins, develop positive feelings and beautiful energies throughout their being – and with an optimum charge of clear attraction, advance towards and suddenly come face to face with that special person they immediately recognize as – their long-desired intimate and mate.

Pause a few moments and reflect: where are you on this continuum? Are you still running wild trying to escape your own self by plunging into another relationship? Have you hit bottom and wallowed in the agony of self-despair and loathing? Are you headed up towards acceptance, self-love and positive but unhurried attraction leading you to your true beloved? Be honest – wherever you find yourself, you now know that you can rapidly move through the first two stages of singing the singles blues, and soon be singing a brighter song of romantic attraction and fulfilment . . . tune into your heart . . . look back on your recent past . . . see where you are, on the path to sexual union and bliss . . .

pause . . . breathe . . . reflect . . . experience

Raising Your Energy

If you realize that you are still caught in the first two stages of singles blues, you will want to spend considerable time working with the programmes in these first three chapters, so that you advance step by step towards healing your heart from old heartbreaks, letting go of negative attitudes and expectations that hold you back from true love, and becoming your own best friend. But even if you're still very much engaged in these essential preparations of the heart for new love, go ahead and read on through the rest of the book now, so that you have a sense of the whole flow of this programme, which is designed to take you all the way from heartbreak to a fulfilling new relationship.

We've so far focused almost entirely on you and your inner needs and yearnings. In the next chapter we're going to expand our discussion and awareness a radical new step, to include the person out there right now who is destined at some point to be the person who becomes your new lover and perhaps life mate. In the scientific logic of this space-time continuum that we all live within, if you are destined to meet this person sometime in the future, then you are already on blissful-collision course. And therefore, you can tune into this person you are destined to meet and spark with right now in this present moment, days or weeks or even years before the actual encounter.

And as soon as you have this sense that there's someone out there that you are going to encounter and spark with, you're ready to begin amping up your charge of attraction energy, so that you can begin focusing this energy in this person's direction. And how do you amp up your attraction energy? Let's begin to answer this question in this chapter, and spend the next few chapters fully exploring its various dimensions.

The energy you feel in your body related to attaining sexual fulfilment expresses itself in the feelings usually labelled as desire, hunger, passion, lust, craving and yearning. Whenever you feel any one of these (they of course overlap) you stimulate the creation of a primal energy that pushes for fulfilment through sexual union, romantic togetherness, and also more long-term mating and family creation.

If you're in the first phase of singles blues, you're probably often consumed with a high energetic charge that might attract someone of similar needing condition into your arms, but as you've probably learned already, when you come together unprepared for deep love, usually the affair comes to a painful end.

If you're in the second phase of singles blues, down in the pits of self-pity, hopelessness and despair, your energy level will be very low, and your power to attract your desired lover likewise very low. I hope that you now see that the best path out of this valley of the shadow of romantic death is through finally throwing off outdated notions about love and romance, healing your own wounds, and preparing yourself for a totally new kind of love, that can truly endure.

As you begin to move out of the pit of romantic despair, and feel good and hopeful again in your heart, you'll naturally begin to feel a renewed sense of lust, passion, yearning, and desire. And at this point, increasing your attraction charge by welcoming these feelings into your everyday life is a very good idea – you're now ready to increase your attraction charge, because as we'll explore in the next chapter, you're ready to aim this charge out into the world, to touch the heart of that person out there who is almost certainly right now going through the same process.

It's been noted in studies of the romantic experience that people tend to team up with people who are on the same stage of the romance journey. This means that right now, the person you're going to meet down the road somewhere is working through the same basic issues and emotional preparations that you are – so that when you come together, you're already in deep synchronization emotionally and growth-wise. Exactly where in your evolution you will come together, God only knows. But you have the power to accelerate your discovery of someone out there of similar resonance through actively, each day, spending time preparing yourself and advancing along the track to heart encounter.

So from here on out, I encourage you to welcome the feelings that have perhaps made you ache in your heart and genitals. Go ahead and encourage a strong charge of yearning and desire in your body – because in the very next chapter, I'm going to begin teaching you how to direct that power of desire in ways that will bring you into heart contact with your lover, not later, but now!

Exercise Four: ENCOURAGING ENERGY

To end this chapter, let me walk you through a basic desire/attraction process that you will want to do regularly from here on out, to encourage the inflow of that powerful charge of energy that mobilizes your attraction potential. At first here, just do this lightly, to explore the process. Later on we'll explore advanced approaches to the basic process. You'll find this experience to be an expansion of the meditation we did earlier on in this chapter – I'm building one process upon the next so that the learning experience is easy for you:

Again, tune into your breathing . . . let it come and go freely for a few breaths . . . and now expand your awareness to include the feelings in your heart . . . open up to all the romantic desires and passions that so often fill your heart . . . and also now tune into your genitals . . . let yourself wake up down there – feel your rising power of sexual hunger and passion . . . and also tune into your power centre in your belly . . . feel your energy increasing, to move soon into action to satisfy your heart's desires . . .

And now expand your awareness to include your tongue . . . your throat . . . your jaw muscles . . . and your lips . . . open your mouth and breathe freely through the mouth and see how this feels to you . . . bite a few times with your teeth to feel that biting reflex in action . . . on your exhales make a few growls . . . smile and growl at the same time, with your mouth wide open as if to bite! . . . and now say out loud (unless you're on the subway of course) – 'I'm hungry for love! . . . I'm hungry for love! . . . I'm hungry – for love!' . . .

And now just relax, breathe freely . . . notice how you feel in your heart . . . in your genitals . . . in your power centre . . . in your throat and mouth . . . and say to yourself, 'I like feeling hungry for love' . . . and with every new inhale breathe in a higher charge of energy . . . and with every exhale, feel your power inside and enjoy it . . . inhale and bring in more attraction power . . . exhale and express your desire to the world . . .and be open to a new feeling of power and pleasure – and joyful anticipation – throughout your body . . .

pause . . . breathe . . . reflect . . . experience

Chapter 5

Broadcast Your Presence – Contact Your Lover

HEART ENCOUNTER – FIVE

Danielle had spent months with the programmes concentrating on somehow recovering her heart from the terrible disaster of her marriage. She had entirely given her life to her husband, only to suddenly have him leave her for a woman who maybe was more sexy, certainly more openly flouting her feminine attributes. Danielle had come from a very conservative religious family and perhaps she'd been slow to begin to have a wild sexual life. And her friends assured her that her husband's new girlfriend was just as shallow as he had turned out to be. But still, the wounds had been almost deadly and she was slow to recover.

This time though, as she finally started considering the possibility of new love in her life, she made sure that she spent time becoming her own best friend rather than depending entirely on a man for her emotional wellbeing. And as she practised meditating on her heart and the inflow of love, she discovered something she considered equally important to any romantic benefit – she came face to face, heart to heart with a spiritual quality to life that she'd always suspected might exist, but had never focused on discovering for herself.

The more she opened her heart to the inflow of spiritual love and guidance, the more she felt independent in her heart, and actually not emotionally needy at all. Where there once had been the agony of loneliness in the evening when she was alone in her apartment, she now had the soft warm sense of being her own best friend, and the rush of inner bliss when she did her meditations and connected with her deeper spiritual source. She felt like she could continue like this forever, but then –

I took my little boy to his pre-school one morning as usual before going to work, and noticed a man dropping his son off at the same time. I hadn't seen this man before, and he was good-looking to me – but when he met my eyes he didn't seem at all interested in me. This happened several times in the next weeks, where we would happen to cross paths at the pre-school, and once at the grocery store, and I would feel a sudden excitement at seeing him, but he again mostly ignored me beyond the formal greetings. I found out that he was, like me, divorced – but not much more.

But in my meditations, I began to tune into his presence and every time I quieted my mind and looked inward to my heart – there Jacob would be! Not only did I see his face in my meditations. More and more, I would feel his heart and sense that I was connected with him. The feeling of love that would flow between our hearts in my meditations was more and more intense, waking me up sexually as well as other ways. Yes, sometimes I'd get such a charge that I'd masturbate thinking of having him inside me – and each time I did that, something exploded inside me that was new, and that I wanted first-person with him.

Then I'd drop my boy off at school the next morning, my heart pounding and my whole body almost trembling with anticipation, assuming Jacob must have also felt the intensity of my sexual vision the night before – I was certain we'd been heart-to-heart and skin-to-skin at some mysterious dimension. But in he'd walk, and even though he'd say hi to me in a friendly way, there was no recognition of anything deeper.

So in my meditations I began to make an even bolder attempt to reach him. I knew in my heart that we were somehow already together, and I would move through the meditation until I felt Jacob's presence in my heart strongly, then say to him as if I was with him, 'I can wait. I don't mean to push into your life - but I can't stop feeling how I do towards you.' And I'd just sit there, filled with love for him, night after night. I admit that this level of togetherness, just at some spiritual level, was very fulfilling. And meanwhile, yes, even though I'd always thought masturbation was somehow wrong, I found myself waking up feelings in myself that I never knew existed, and that self-exploration sexually was somehow very very important to me right then . . .

Easter was approaching. The little school put on a simple play, and afterwards we stood around talking, and even though I'm usually somewhat shy, I found myself walking right up to Jacob, who I realized was likewise quite shy. Our two boys were playing together, and we stood a moment watching them play. Then with no forethought I blurted out, 'We're going out into the country for a hike tomorrow, would you two like to come along?'

He looked at me as if I'd said something wrong, and frowned. 'Oh, well – I don't know,' he said.

'Jacob, is it that you just don't like me? Because if it is, I'll just leave you alone.'

He glared at me in reaction. 'I didn't say I don't like you.'

'No, you just act like it.'

'That's not true.'

"So then, I'm asking you if you'd like to spend some time with us tomorrow. It's that simple, yes or no, I just thought I'd ask.'

He looked at me with eyes that were suddenly liquid. 'Uhm,' he hesitated, 'I'm not sure. Can I phone you?'

'Sure, phone me,' I said, and walked away from him, taking my boy by the hand, my ears burning with embarrassed emotion as I left the room. And of course there I sat that evening, feeling like a teenager hopelessly in love. Had my heart been entirely wrong, did this whole attraction meditation thing not work at all? Here I was for the first time in my life, seriously aflame with desire for a man and ready to share that passion utterly – and the jerk wasn't even phoning me to say no. I'd played the impossible role for me and actually asked a man out on a date – and he wasn't even bothering to phone to reject my offer.

The phone rang. My little boy answered it in his cute voice and handed it to me.

'Danielle,' a male voice said, 'it's me – Jacob.'

'Oh.'

'I was, uhm, a bit shocked by your offer at school.'

'Shocked?' I reacted. 'There was nothing shocking in the offer, just a walk in the woods.'

'Well, it's not just that,' he said, and hesitated.

'Oh – so what is it then?'

'It's just that – Danielle, I've got to say this.'

'Alright then,' I told him, my heart crashing. 'Say it.'

'It's just that I've been trying to get up the nerve to ask you out for weeks now. How embarrassing to have you ask me first.'

I was silent a moment, my heart suddenly pounding loud in my ears. 'Well,' I told him, still defensive, 'you certainly never showed any overt interest in me. You've been cold as stone.'

Another silence. I was hardly breathing at all. 'The first time I saw you,' he said, 'your hair, it's the same as my wife's was. When I saw you from behind, at first I thought you were her. And ever since, I've been saying to myself, no, stop this, you can't fall in love with someone who looks like your ex-wife.'

I didn't have anything to say to that – or rather I had a hundred things to say at once, and ended up not saying any of them. Instead, a wave of relief coming over me, I told him, 'I'm sure I can prove to you quite effectively that I'm not your ex-wife.'

'Yes,' he said. 'Yes. It's just stupid – but . . . please, I want to spend time with you.'

Not only did he let me rapidly prove that I wasn't his ex-wife, in seven months he took me as his new wife . . .

Once you progress a bit with the first chapters, preparing your heart and soul for a new lover, you're ready to also begin the next giant step in this process – learning to actively broadcast your heart presence and contact your lover heart to heart. As mentioned in the introduction, my own primary experience with this broadcast-contact process was so dramatic, at first I could hardly believe what I felt in my heart – the living presence of another human being 'with me' even though I was still alone. But that experience was definitely real – because as I trusted that feeling, and allowed it to guide me to come closer to that person out there who had contacted me, we did indeed find each other.

In this chapter, let's explore in more depth not only how science can now explain such a 'distance-contact' experience, but also how you can actively begin, right now, to encourage this experience yourself, in your own heart. The pay-off is immense, because you go from feeling alone (and probably lonely) to feeling you're in contact with someone out there, and therefore no longer alone (nor lonely).

For thousands of years, human beings have expressed what was considered an esoteric belief that they can commune with like-hearted souls from a distance – sometimes even halfway around the world. In similar mode people have spoken in religious terms of having Jesus in their hearts, or Buddha, or another enlightened spiritual being who seems to transcend even time, to make heart contact with us. Now we have the scientific proof that indeed, our intuitive hunches and deep heart feelings have been valid.

Specifically, research into the power of the human mind to influence the performance of sensitive machines at a distance, has been proven. Likewise the power of the mind to project images and ideas and basic emotions into another person's mind and heart has been documented beyond a question of a doubt, in long-term studies such as Princeton University's Engineering Anomalies Research. As Robert Jahn, dean emeritus of the Princeton School of Engineering and Applied Science and head of the Engineering Anomalies Programme which conducted this new research, states it: 'In order to comprehend this new understanding of the impact of consciousness on environment, nothing less than a generously expanded model of reality will be required, one that allows consciousness a proactive role in the establishment of its experience of the physical world. Integration of these changes in our worldview can lead to a substantially superior cultural ethic, wherein the long-estranged siblings of science and spirit will be productively reunited.'

This statement by a renowned scientist is almost shocking, because it lays out the vast shift in our sense of who we are and what we can do, both romantically and in general, with the power of our own minds and hearts. Now when I say to you, let's learn how to use the power of your own mind and heart to broadcast your presence to like-minded people, and attract them to you, I'm proposing not just a wonderful magical mystic experience, but a process grounded in the new science.

Throughout history, as you probably know, many of our wisest scholars and scientists have openly claimed that they could sense the presence of an invisible yet almost palpable power of attraction and manifestation that exists within their own minds. Sir Isaac Newton, that patriarch of classic Western science, stated clearly that for him the primary force of change in the world would prove to be 'the mystery by which mind could control matter'. Francis Bacon, Elizabethan father of the experimental method, was highly interested in studying such 'mind over matter' phenomena as telepathic dreams, psychic healing, transmission of thoughts, and the power of the mind on the casting of dice. And more recently, great names in contemporary physics such as Max Planck, Niels Bohr, Albert Einstein, Werner Heisenberg, Erwin Schrödinger, and David Bohm have all written about the still-mysterious influence of consciousness on external matter and events.

However, only recently has our experimental method become sharp enough technologically to know how to test the driving question of whether or not the human mind can broadcast actual energetic information beyond the physical body, and statistically impact the world and other people's consciousness from a distance. The last twenty years have been landmark decades for consciousness research. Any number of studies could be cited from around the world, but perhaps the first and by now most solid set of studies demonstrating the actual scientific presence and behaviour of consciousness is that begun in 1979 by Robert Jahn at the traditionally quite conservative Princeton School of Engineering and Applied Science. In a book such as this, we won't go extensively into the fine points of this research. Please go online to my website at www.johnselby.com to access the research data.

Basically, Professor Jahn and team proved that you yourself have a mental power whose effects can be measured with experimental instruments at a distance. Your thoughts, and your heart's intent, do broadcast out into the world with a very subtle but effective power. And when properly focused towards a receptive person, your thoughts and feelings can influence the thoughts and feelings of someone you are focusing intently upon. This is no longer a fantasy of mystic folk – this is proven scientific fact. I was at Princeton when these studies were begun, and have followed them to their conclusion with great interest, and am very pleased to bring this research into mainstream discussion because as Jahn said above, this discovery does strongly impact our basic sense of who we are, and how such things as heart-to-heart distance communion, and love at first sight, do very realistically happen.

Our challenge here is to learn how to use our hearts and minds to maximize our broadcast in such a way that very special people will tune into our broadcast and make heart contact that will lead to physical encounter at some future point.

A New Sense of Sharing Space

Once the initial Princeton Study was completed, showing that the human mind can influence the performance of a sensitive computer a few feet away, the experimenters moved the computer farther and farther away from the mental broadcaster, expecting the effect to diminish. But to their surprise, even when the computer was actually moved from Princeton to Tokyo, the effects remained constant. Distance was not a factor in this mental broadcast power – amazing but true.

The implications of this discovery in your search for your new lover are dramatic. If right now, the person you're going to meet and team up with at a future date is in another country, this doesn't matter at all. You can still broadcast your presence, and touch this person's heart – and likewise you can receive and be touched by this special person's presence, no matter where this person is broadcasting from. I was in Berlin and my future mate was in Switzerland when we first made contact. Then, responding to the inner pull, I allowed myself to take a trip down to Switzerland – but she went on her vacation to Italy. Sensing that I was closer to her than before, and feeling certain that she was coming in my direction, I stayed overlong in Switzerland for three extra days, just waiting – while she cancelled the last days of her Italian vacation, feeling pulled home – and finally we met . . .

We had felt like we were sharing space for several weeks before we came physically together. And we had got to know the 'feel' of each other's presence from a distance, so that when we were suddenly face to face, it was like we definitely already knew each other. This is the experience I'm helping you learn how to nurture in this chapter, and in the rest of this book – that sense of right now, beginning to tune into the presence of your future lover, so that you can come together at subtle heart and mind dimensions that we now know scientifically as well as intuitively there exist.

Does opening up to this experience interest you? Probably the scientific research is new to you – do you believe it's true? Let's pause so that you can breathe into the notion that you have the power to broadcast your presence and your intent, so that other like-minded and resonant people can pick up your broadcast, and respond with their own broadcast – are you ready to begin this very exciting process of attraction from a distance?

pause ... breathe ... reflect ... experience

Heart Contact and The Time Factor

Naturally the scientists running the Princeton Study began asking themselves, 'If the mind has the power to transmit energetic information and intent over distance, then what about over time?' Professor Jahn realized that the broadcast coming from the human mind and energetic body must be some kind of wave pattern, travelling through some as-yet-unidentified medium. If this broadcast functioned outside the distance/space dimension of the space-time continuum, did it also function outside the temporal dimension of the space-time continuum? A scary idea, but for thousands of years mystics have spoken of having heart contact with their spiritual teachers even if those spiritual teachers had left the earth hundreds and even thousands of years before – it was certainly worth experimenting to find out.

Again, truly startling results were obtained – the factor of time between stimulus and response didn't diminish the broadcaster's mental ability to influence the performance of the computer. Somehow the medium through which the conscious intent was broadcast stored this information until the computer was turned on and the study run. And likewise it now seems scientifically clear that if we send out our broadcast in our daily attraction meditation, people of similar heart and mind and personal presence can receive this broadcast when they stop and tune in, even if the timing isn't congruent. Your welcoming broadcast of love, acceptance and desire remains in the air, so to speak, awaiting reception.

Similar studies have shown that when two people know each other and feel empathy and resonance towards each other, one person can think a particular shape or colour or broadcast a particular feeling in the heart, and the other person, regardless of distance or timing, can tune in and pick up this broadcast at statistically valid levels of probability. This means that if you are clear in your daily meditation of your intent, and also of your position physically in your country, town and street, this information can be received at subtle levels in the other person's mind, and influence decisions about where to go that day, and what plans to make for travel in the near future.

Again, I'm not asking you to believe what I'm telling you. My intent here is to share with you the actual reality of the situation we're talking about together, as best I have come to understand it. Your response will be to entertain the new ideas, and experiment in your own heart and mind with the process we're learning, and see how it works for you.

Pause again, and just for a moment, see how it feels to consider spending time each day doing the attraction meditation I'm going to teach you, and actively broadcasting your desires and location out into the world. Also, imagine sitting quietly one or more times each new day, to open your heart and mind and soul to receive broadcasts from like-minded souls who are seeking someone like you . . .

pause . . . breathe . . . reflect . . . experience

Like-Minded Souls Attracting

The Princeton Studies show that the broadcasts we send out into the world do need to be aimed with a power of intent that directs the broadcast where we want it to have strong impact. Carl Jung was apparently right in his thesis a hundred years ago that there exists a 'collective unconscious' consisting of all our broadcasts of ideas and feelings throughout the world. And yes, we can tune into this general vast presence of human intent and pick up broadcasts that resonate with our own interests and understandings. But mostly we're unaware, day in and day out, of the broadcasts of everyone around us – except to the extent that we live within a general mutual feeling of belonging to the larger circle of humanity, and participating in the general intent of our culture.

If we want to employ the power of mutual attraction to our direct benefit, we need to first of all be clear as to who we are and who we're seeking – and broadcast a clear signal regularly out into the world, that like-minded souls can pick up and respond to. In the same way that you don't want to attract the wrong people to you sexually when you're walking down the street or at a party, you don't want to attract the wrong people at these more subtle levels either. Many people are unclear or downright confused regarding who they really need to team up with in their lives – and thus end up attracting idealized images or fanciful lovers into their arms, with disastrous results.

In the same way, as mentioned before, many people believe (from past romantic programming and religious assumptions) that there's only one true soul mate out there in the world for them – just one human being out of six or seven billion whom they are destined to meet and mate with. If you have this ingrained belief, please at least consider the possibility that it's too limiting a concept for realistic encounter with someone you're compatible with.

As a psychologist and marriage counsellor I can assure you that you are romantically compatible with more than one of the six billion human beings to choose from. I experienced this very vividly during the months before I finally met my one true love. As I became more and more happy with my own self, as I learned to let love flow into my heart more and more, and as I became more and more clear as to who I was seeking, I seemed to begin to attract more and more women into my life who were possible mates. Just in the flash of an eye on the subway I would find someone looking at me who looked familiar, with whom I resonated – and with whom I might possibly come together.

As my heart began resonating with a loud clear signal that I was ready, that I was clear, and that I was strong on my own two feet and not seeking a co-dependent relationship, more and more women of similar resonance seemed to start appearing in my life. I was lighter on my feet because I was singing a happy song and already feeling heart-to-heart with my new lover. Everywhere I ventured, I knew I could run into her and – pow! And in this state of alert love and expectation, I seemed to be encountering one possible mate after another.

The most interesting aspect of this state of mind and body that I more and more entered into as I approached my fated encounter with my true love, was that I became quite relaxed and confident, and less and less needy. Life was good, I already felt in love – I just hadn't come physically into contact with her yet. And I am confident in my heart that if I hadn't come together with the woman I did, I would have come together with a similar woman, unique but highly compatible with me, with whom I would have been equally happy and satisfied, as I am with my wife. I don't say this in any way to reduce the vast infinite satisfaction and pleasure and compatibility that she and I have shared these last twenty years. I simply want to make it clear that I realized then, and acknowledge now, that there are many women with whom I could be very satisfied with as a life mate. There is a bountiful abundance of potential mates for us all in this world. The singles problem isn't lack of available mates – our problem rather is lack of preparation and inner healing required for successful mating.

What is your present opinion about what we're talking over here – do you feel there's only one true love out there for you, and you have to find him or her in the stack of six billion? Or can you open your heart to the presence of hundreds, perhaps thousands of like-minded folk out there – people who are like you, who have needs similar to yours and yearnings parallel with yours, who are right now hungering to meet someone just like you . . . look to your heart right now, and see if you're ready to open your heart to actually feel these similar people, and let them feel your presence – right now!

pause . . . breathe . . . reflect . . . experience

A Simple Matter Of Resonance

So there is someone out there in that mass of billions of human beings on this planet, who can make you happy and fulfil your every desire. The challenge is to use every means available to find that person, initiate your relationship, and carry forth for however long you're fated to be together. I would also like to say that we never know, when we enter into a relationship, how long that relationship will last. If loving someone unconditionally means letting them go when their path needs to diverge from yours, then you can't insist that this new lover stay with you the rest of your life. That's a wonderful possibility – but as we'll see later on, true love means being ready to let go, if and when that time comes to go your separate ways. If you can accept this dimension of romance, you can truly give all your heart and soul – and be able to reclaim your independent status if required.

What means do you have available, for finding a lover with whom you can feel satisfied and happy?

1. You have the ability to move around in new places, and break old life routines so that you encounter new people – we'll get into that process later on;
2. You have the ability to upgrade and clarify your genuine needs regarding who you're looking for, so that your perceptions are clear and ready to identify like-minded folk when they appear. We're in the process of accomplishing that goal;
3. You have the ability to heal old heart wounds and unrealistic romantic notions, so that you're prepared emotionally for a satisfying relationship – you're learning how to do this already;
4. You have the ability and power to fine-tune your heart's yearnings and your whole-body energetic radiations, and begin to broadcast a loud and clear signal that will attract like-minded people to you, regardless of where they might be right now on the planet;
5. And – you have (or will have shortly) the capacity to use your heart and mind as a receiver of broadcasts from like-minded

folk, so that you have a two-way experience happening between you to step-by-step guide you physically into each other's arms.

Let's focus now on items four and five, as we now begin your formal training in the heart broadcast biz. Much of what we've talked about in earlier chapters will certainly be required preparation for operating a successful broadcast system, and I trust that once you've read through all this book a first time, you'll return to the preparation exercises in earlier chapters. But even if you're just beginning to work with the programmes for healing old emotional wounds and preparing your heart for true love, you can also begin mastering the fine art of using your heart and energetic body for broadcasting and receiving the vital information needed to attract your new lover.

You are a human being with a wide variety of feelings in your heart and throughout your body. As we've seen, these feelings are actually of an energetic nature, and research shows these feelings can be broadcast out into the world in such a way that someone 'out there' can pick up, in his or her own energetic body, your broadcasts – and experience them! You've surely had such experiences already, when you felt empathy for something someone was feeling, or simply felt the loving presence of someone in your heart. Yes, you can stimulate such feelings through memory and imagination – but we now know that you can also directly receive and experience another person's emanations.

Why is it that you can tune into a particular person's presence at a distance and 'feel' this person in your heart, while remaining unaware of the emotional broadcasts of literally billions of other people? It seems clear that we are most sensitive to receiving broadcasts from people with whom we feel a certain similar resonance in the heart – people we are similar to at basic energetic levels. Resonance is a key word in understanding and applying the principles of attraction we're exploring here, so let's go a step deeper into a clear sense of what resonance is all about between two hearts and souls.

Professor Jahn completed a most interesting related study that demonstrated how two people who are in a positive sexual relation-ship, when paired in doing the broadcast experiment, generated not twice the effect (as would be expected) but a full six times the effect. Somehow, just by changing the one variable of romantic resonance, three times the power was generated in the combined power of intent. No wonder we feel more alive, more powerful, more integrated when we're in love – somehow the combination of our two resonances into one greater intent amplifies our power considerably, giving our combined intent greater effect than if we were alone.

And even before you meet with your true love, my experience is that as soon as you begin with a daily or twice-daily attraction meditation routine (as we'll learn in later chapters) you tune into a considerable number of like-minded resonances out there in the world – and all of you benefit through the integration of your similar desires and intent. You all become more powerful. The same thing happens when you do a formal spiritual meditation and tune into the presence of God in your life. You increase your resonance through resonating with the presence of love in the universe. This is such a massive theme in itself that I've devoted an entire book called *Seven Masters, One Path*, to its explor-ation at more spiritual realms of discussion.

After completing almost twenty years of research into this and related studies, Professor Jahn has concluded that 'there exists no distinct boundary between mind and matter at the wave/particle level of reality. Instead, consciousness permeates outward into its surrounding environment to an extent consistent with its prevailing purpose'. In all the studies, the intent of the broadcaster and receiver in an experiment determines the nature and success of the experi-ment. Distance and time aren't factors – but the quality and intensity of intent most certainly are. The same will be true in the success of your romantic broadcasts – the quality and clarity and intensity of your resonance determines everything.

Professor Jahn noted for instance, that the presence of human feelings of empathy and bondedness were crucial in the experiments. Even when relating with a computer, if the experimenter felt anthropomorphic feelings towards the computer, as if relating with a human being heart to heart, the effects were noticeably higher. So it's not just the thoughts you think related to your intent, that determine your broadcast power, it's surely the emotions that you hold in your heart that empower your broadcast.

And what determines who out there will be most liable to be sensitive to your broadcast, and feel it in their hearts? The key term researchers in the quantum mechanics of consciousness use to explain the experience of heart contact from a distance (or indeed when you're very close) is the word *resonance*, which they formally define as any situation wherein 'one object (or person) is of such similar constitution so as to begin resonating at the same frequency when encountering the vibration of another object (or person)'.

Said in lay terms, resonance is the inherent capacity of two different things or people to vibrate in harmony with each other. The classic example is that of a wine glass beginning to vibrate at the same pitch an opera singer is singing, generating a sound at the same frequency being sung. Two people of like mind (people with harmonious personalities broadcasting the same basic energetic/emotional/conceptual intent) become linked to each other through this mutual resonance, and progressively are drawn to each other physically.

The only way scientists can make sense of this ability of one person to broadcast to and contact another person, even over thousands of miles and in different time frames, is to assume that both parties are living within what is called 'a single interactive system' – an expanded transpersonal consciousness which includes both parties. Jahn speaks of the experience of being in love as 'a process of wave-mechanical resonance between two components of a single interactive system'. When you share love with a similar-minded person, you join together in a unique 'single interactive system' that comes into being when the two of you are in resonance. When both of you put your attention on a common desire or feeling, a current of energy is generated between the two of you and it – and you merge into one greater awareness.

Here's a beginning taste of the experience we're talking about. Think for a few moments of someone you already know and love, be this your mother or a friend, brother or sister or spiritual master or whomever – choose someone you love and who loves you – and begin to focus your mind's attention and your heart's feelings of love in the direction of this person . . . and as you breathe into the good feelings of love and acceptance that you share with this person, experience the actual sense of contact, the feeling of being bonded with this person, your two hearts resonating with the same good feeling towards each other . . . and to increase the feeling, say to this person, 'I love you,' a few times, and notice how this direct statement amplifies your sense of resonance with this person . . .

pause . . . breathe . . . reflect . . . experience

Receive Mode

Along with actively broadcasting your love out into the world in the specific direction you want to send it, your final variable in romantic success is your dedication to the act of opening up to receive someone else's broadcast. Yes, there is someone out there who is looking for someone just like you. And yes, one way or another (if you two are ever going to come together) this person is not only opening to receive your love broadcast, but is also actively sending out his or her love broadcast.

Are you conscious of the presence of broadcasts coming your way, and are you eager to be receptive to them – to be touched in your heart? Specifically, have you prepared a place in your heart for this new person? And do you regularly pause meditatively to open up and receive the broadcasts that are being aimed in the direction of people just like you?

Many lonely people crave affection yet shut themselves off to being found by people who could give them affection. Often people get hurt in love, and then just shut down entirely so as not to be hurt again. They might yearn tragically for new love, but they'll never be found by a new love if they're habitually closed off in their hearts to the experience of that sudden feeling of heart resonance when someone out there is broadcasting in their direction. How do you rate yourself in this regard – are you open to being touched anew? Reflect on how you might answer each of the following:

'I hunger for new love to come into my life.'

'I'm afraid of love.'

'My heart is wide open to be touched by someone new.'

'I'm mostly closed down and afraid of a new sexual encounter.'

'I feel confidant that the right person will soon come my way.'

'I've been hurt too much to trust again.'

'True love only comes once in a lifetime.'

'There are plenty of potential lovers out there awaiting me.'

'I won't let anybody into my heart again.'

'My heart is open . . . to receive new love.'

Please do hold in mind, if you find your present attitudes somewhat contracted in your answers above, that we're in a process of healing here – you wouldn't be reading this book if you didn't acknowledge that you have at least a few romance issues to resolve and move beyond, in order to prepare yourself for a good solid new relationship. Even if you read the sentence 'I've been hurt too much to trust again' and find a part of you that agrees with the statement, the very process of realizing that you have a hurt frightened part of you that needs loving attention, is part of your emotional recovery and re-emergence into the ultimately magnificent game of love.

I'm here to show you how to heal your heart, and prepare room for new love as you forgive and move on beyond your old love affairs. You're here to learn how to go through that preparation process, to actively attract new love into your life – and then succeed with that new love when it comes.

Let's see what happens when you shift into receive mode. You'll remember earlier I offered you the magic focus phrase, 'My heart is open to receive the inflow of love.' Love can come from God, from your father, from an old friend or a new colleague – or even from your faithful dog or orangutan. To open up in general to the inflow of love is perhaps the most essential act you can make in life, if indeed as the Beatles assured us, 'love is all there is'. To feel loved is to feel alive and good and in resonance with the greater loving presence of God in all his and her glorious manifestations.

What we're now preparing to do is to fine-tune your openness to receive love – so that you filter out all the general broadcasts coming your way, and focus upon those that are coming from people with the following similarities of resonance and intent:

1. People hungry for love but emotionally solid on their own two feet.
2. People seeking the same basic kind of sex you're seeking.
3. People with whom you strongly resonate personality-wise.
4. People with the same basic values and sensibilities as you.
5. People you'll be attracted to and take great pleasure in sexually.
6. People as ready for deep lasting love as you are.
7. People with the same basic romantic intent as yours.

Right at this moment, maybe there are a thousand people out there who match these seven basic requirements that you place on who you'll let into your heart. Maybe there are a million – they're out there. The question is, are you ready to open up and feel their loving presence in your heart? If not, fine, like I said – we're in process here. And there's plenty of time. Read down the list again please, and this time, stay aware of your breathing, and your heart – and while you're aware of the feelings in your heart right now, say each of the requirements, and reflect on each in turn:

pause ... breathe ... reflect ... experience

Let Love Find You

So many single people I meet are suffering from extreme agony emotionally, because they feel no love in their hearts – they feel empty, unloved and unloving. This suffering is terrible, I know, I've been there. What we're doing here is side-stepping that agony altogether by actively opening our hearts to let love flow in, and actively broadcasting our love out to those who resonate with our own feelings and desires in life.

Attitude is all. What you believe is what you get in life. The thoughts you run through your mind determine the experience that comes to you. We've discussed these truths in earlier chapters. Now let's apply them directly to whether you're hiding from love, or actively opening to let love find you. Again, focus phrases that resonate throughout your being can work wonders.

Say each sentence below in turn, and see if you resonate with the words – and be open to a new insight or experience:

ONE: I am here right now, alive and ready for love.

TWO: There is someone out there I want to meet and love.

THREE: I have the power to reach out with my heart and contact this person.

FOUR: I'm open to feel contact with this person, directly in my heart.

FIVE: I am ready to begin the process of attracting this person into my life.

SIX: I accept that there are many potential mates for me.

SEVEN: I feel part of a resonant group of potential lovers.

EIGHT: My heart feels good, and open to love.

On a scale of one to ten, where ten means you're totally acceptant and ready for what those eight statements presented, it doesn't matter if you're a two or an eight or whatever. What matters is that you're focusing your power of intent right now, on advancing towards a ten on each of the statements. Your own internal pressures of desire, yearning and even craving are the fuel that will move you step by step to where all this makes sense, and you're doing it – and it happens. I encourage you to enjoy each step along the path – this present moment is golden because every bit of new love that you open up and let flow into your heart will make you feel better, and that good feeling will help you to heal and advance another step . . .

Exercise Five: THE ATTRACTION MEDITATION

Let me lead you now through the basic attraction meditation that you'll be mastering and applying at least once a day in your Let Love Find You ceremony. Rest assured that we'll be fine-tuning your ability to move successfully through this process in later chapters as well. Read through the process once, then return and go more deeply into each step. Remember that you can also go online and hear my voice guiding you through this when you want to:

Set aside five to ten minutes when you have plenty of time to relax . . . and find a comfortable place to do this attraction meditation. Make sure you're feeling good in your body to start out with – feel free to stretch all your want, and to yawn . . . let your body move as it wants to, so as to discharge tensions.

Tune into the air flowing in and out your nose (or mouth) as you breathe . . . expand your awareness to include the movements in your chest and belly as your breaths come and go and come again . . . and gently expand your awareness to include the feelings in your heart, right in the middle of your breathing. Accept whatever feelings you find right now, breathe into them, let them change with each new breath . . .

Expand your awareness to include your whole body, here in this present moment. Be aware of your toes . . . your hands . . . your throat . . . your pelvis . . . your knees . . . your belly . . . and allow your awareness to move around your body and find places that feel especially good right now . . . enjoy the good feelings you find . . .

move all you want to let these good feelings expand . . .

And now relax . . . bring your focus to your breathing again . . . and the feeling in your heart . . . and begin to think of someone whom you love. Let your love for this person fill your heart as you aim your attention towards this person, wherever they may be – they can feel your attention when you aim it towards them . . . they can feel your love . . . enjoy this heart-to-heart communion a few moments . . .

And now shift into receive mode in your heart, so that you begin to feel the love this person has for you . . . open your heart, and let their love come in . . . and open your heart more as you let all the pure spiritual love of the universe come flowing into your heart . . . with every new breath, be open to receive more love, until your whole heart and being is full of love . . . relax and enjoy this loving feeling . . .

And now return your attention to your breaths coming and going . . . and let's begin to focus specifically on your yearning for a new deep love in your life . . . say to yourself the following five focus sentences, to help tune your intent where you want it focused:

> *'I am here right now, alive and ready for love.'*
> *'There is someone out there I am going to meet*
>   *and love.'*
> *'I have the power to reach out with my heart and*
>   *contact this person.'*
> *'I'm open to experience resonance with this person,*
>   *directly in my heart.'*
> *'I am ready to begin the process of attracting this*
>   *person into my life.'*

Just relax . . . breathe freely . . . feel your desire for your new lover growing strongly in your heart . . . also feel this desire down in your sexual centre where you hunger to share sexual attraction, stimulation, excitation, and erotic release . . . expand your awareness to include your power centre in your belly where you feel rising energy to actively get out and find your lover . . . expand your awareness to include your throat and mouth . . . relax your jaw, and breathe through the mouth as you sigh . . . experience your passion for your new lover filling your whole body . . . enjoy your charge of energy . . . breathe into it . . . let it fill you and begin to flow outward – towards your lover!

Say in your heart, to your lover, *'Here I am, reaching out to touch you . . . feel who I am, come into my heart . . . experience my unique presence . . . receive my love.'*

Hold your focus on the person out there who will be the one you will meet and love. Breathe deeply and with every exhale, say directly to this person, *'I love you . . . I want you . . . we're moving towards each other . . .'*

After you have broadcast your love and presence and romantic intent out towards your coming lover for ten to twenty breaths, you can now just relax . . . let your breaths come and go on their own . . . be open to a new experience in your heart . . . and now begin to receive your lover's broadcast, as you open your heart to let love flow in . . . Say to yourself, *'My heart is open, to receive your love . . . I can feel you . . . I wake up in passion and desire for you . . . here I am . . . come find me!'*

After ten to twenty breaths of being open to receive love and feel passion and resonate heart-to-heart with your new lover, just relax again and bring your awareness back to your breaths coming . . . and going . . . as you enjoy the new feelings in your heart – of being connected . . . of being in touch . . . of resonating on all levels, sexual and spiritual, with your lover.

You can hold this feeling of connectedness strongly in your heart, so that every move you make, every decision you make, every step you take moves you closer towards this person . . . you are now actively attracting each other . . . soon you will find yourselves so close that you look in each other's eyes – and know you have found each other!

When you're ready, you can open your eyes if they're closed . . .

stretch a little . . . and end this attraction meditation . . . and as you go about your day with your heart filled with a special love, your whole body will feel alive with the anticipation of coming closer to and being intimate with your new love . . .

pause . . . breathe . . . reflect . . . experience

Chapter 6

Employ Your Mind's Higher Attraction Powers

HEART ENCOUNTER – SIX

Lisa was one of those lucky girls who had good looks and a smart mind and a friendly disposition, and she sailed through high school with nice boyfriends, good grades and a hopeful attitude about the future. She didn't get into the university she'd dreamed of attending, though – and for the first time it seemed her luck had run out as she went to another university and plodded through four uneventful years of classes. She had boyfriends but never found someone special to fill her life with love. A short love affair would boost her spirits – but when it ended, she'd spiral down into loneliness. Here's how she describes how her life progressed, from that low point:

I hadn't really found a career that excited me in college, so I took whatever job I could find when I graduated, and it was terribly dull. I had a boyfriend and then separated from him. Then I lost that job when the company down-sized, and had to actually move back into my parents' house. It seemed that nothing was opening up in my life. An old friend did her best to brighten me up, and showed me how to meditate, which helped some. I found another regular job and settled into a routine of driving half an hour to and from work, living with my parents – it wasn't at all what I'd dreamed of but I found pleasure in little things. My friend also taught me the Attraction Meditation and each day became more interesting as I kept my spirits up with my growing faith that my life was just perfect as it was. I felt more and more love beginning to flow, just in my everyday encounters with people, and spiritually in my heart, I could feel that I wasn't so alone after all, at deeper levels of things.

Then one morning I woke up – and the electricity was temporarily off in the house. While my dad tried to find the problem I dressed and banged my knee hard against a chair – ouch! I was going to be late for work so I didn't have breakfast even though I was hungry. Then, I got caught speeding through a stop light. Ten minutes later I had to take a long detour around an auto accident, way out into the countryside - and then my car broke down. I flipped open my cell phone to call for some help – and the battery was dead.

By that time my patience was entirely gone, I was ready to scream – but then, as I stood there realizing I couldn't force the world to be the way I wanted it to be, I looked over across an open field . . . and there was the sun rising up out of the autumn mist – and it was so beautiful, all I could do was relish the sight, and give a prayer for being alive and healthy right at that moment –

A new big van pulled over in front of my old clunker and a young man in casual clothes came walking towards me, asking what was wrong. I took a deep breath, met his eyes – and told him nothing was wrong at all, it's such a beautiful morning that my car decided to break down so I would finally stop long enough to enjoy a sunrise.

He laughed at that, and paused to look at the beauty of the morning with me. 'Me neither,' he confessed, 'I haven't stopped long enough to enjoy nature at all, for months.'

We finally looked fully into each other's eyes – for so long that at some point we both turned bashfully back to the sunrise. I could feel his presence intensely beside me. 'Well I owe your car some thanks too,' he said finally. 'I was in such a bad mood five minutes ago, life wasn't fun at all this morning. Everything went wrong, you can't imagine.'

I laughed. 'Oh yes I can,' I told him.

A moment of unexpected, intense intimacy hit us and we both looked away – enjoying the sunrise for a few more moments. Birds were chirping all around us. A couple of beautiful sleek horses raised their heads to watch us watching them. Then his cell phone beeped and he went into action, telling someone that he couldn't help being late to the shoot, he was aiding a fair damsel in distress and chivalry always comes first. He finished his conversation and grinned at me.

'My problem is I have to shoot some stills in twenty minutes,' he confided in me, 'and my assistant phoned in sick so I don't have free time to take you anywhere,' he said. 'But hey – how would you like to come with me and help set up the shoot? That is, if you don't have anything better to do, which I hope you don't because, well, I like you – what say? Ill get a tow truck for your car.'

I thought of my boring job awaiting me and shrugged my shoulders, again risking looking directly into those greeny-blue eyes of his. He seemed full of fun in spite of the pressures on him, and throwing caution to the wind, I grinned back – 'Give me your cell phone,' I told him.

My boss was unhappy but accepted that I wasn't coming into work that day. I grabbed my purse and jumped into the van with this complete stranger – and off we went to his shoot, whatever that was going to be.

A week later I was formally Ronald's assistant and making double what I'd been making before. At university I'd studied graphic design and Ron found my talents quite valuable in his media work, and suddenly I had a job that was satisfying. But the job meant nothing compared to the man I was working with on that job. When I look back, I can't quite believe how effortless it all was, as we drove off together, windows down to the cool air, not really saying all that much, still caught mutually in the effect the sunrise had had on our souls.

He ordered me around like crazy that day, while he worked like crazy to take very special photos of a very special young celebrity lady. She invited us to lunch and before I knew it, I was entirely inside a new world where people talked about things that interested me, and listened when I expressed my views. Ron and I left the lady's home feeling bright and breezy, and ended up in the late afternoon over at a lake watching that same sun we'd seen rise out of the mist, sink down into the mist . . .

He dropped me back at my parents' home around ten. We stood on the doorstep like I used to stand on that same doorstep with early boyfriends, and chatted, holding hands. Something had happened – we'd recognized each other. And I was scheduled to work with him at his office in the city the next day. Since my car wasn't going to be ready, he was going to come by and pick me up. It was twenty minutes out of his way but he grinned that wonderful grin of his and said he'd drive across the whole continent to pick me up. And indeed, as things turned out, I'm sure if I ever asked him to take that continent drive for me, he would.

Late that evening I sat alone in my bedroom meditating. There was nothing but rejoicing and thanks in my heart towards whatever higher powers had brought me together with Ronald. It seemed like a dream as I looked back on the day, and yet it had all unfolded so perfectly and without any effort, as if, yes, it was destined to happen. And to be honest, I'm quite certain it was . . . there's a flow to life that's greater than we can conceive of. And that flow brought me Ron.

T hose of you who have read my other books know that my professional approach integrates both psychological and spiritual understandings of who we are, into a greater whole that is now being referred to as the 'psychospiritual continuum'. Most people, including scientists who reject traditional religious notions of what life is all about, continue to acknowledge that science takes us only so far when it comes to the mystery of human consciousness, and the deeper nature of reality in general.

We can look with experimental equipment only a certain focal distance into the mechanics of life, before we reach the materialist limits of the scientific method – and encounter beyond the mechanics of life, the magic of life. My personal approach to understanding who we are and how we function is to be fervently scientific as far as science takes my exploration – but then to continue the exploration with the other primal exploratory tool we possess, our own inner perception of life. The part of the mystery that we can objectively identify, manipulate, duplicate and explain through the employment of the scientific method, represents the psychological foundation of my work. The part of the mystery that has not yet been clarified by the scientific method but which I know through direct inner experience to exist nonetheless, represents the spiritual foundation of my work.

If you react negatively to any mention at all of the dimensions of life beyond the materialist, feel free to skip over this chapter. The programmes in this book will work just fine if you don't resonate with spiritual discussions. However, if you are intrigued by the universal human experience that there does exist a dimension to life which is beyond our usual three-dimensional materialist experience of the sensory world, I'd like to explore with you several insights that have come to make great sense to me, regarding the deeper aspects of how two people of similar resonance and intent, somehow suddenly come face to face, recognize each other instantly, and experience 'love at first sight'.

Although I took my therapy degree through a different psychological tradition, I've always felt a deep bond with the therapeutic tradition of Carl Jung, the Swiss psychotherapist and spiritual teacher who broke away from Sigmund Freud to develop a unique and invaluable approach to therapy called Jungian Analysis. Jung was blessed with a mind and heart that openly embraced the infinite experiential mystery that lies beyond our scientific method. And he was brave enough to stand up and insist that his inner experience of life was as valid and as real as any external experiment. He insisted that in order to fully encompass the human condition, professionals must expand their vista to include a spiritual dimension.

Jung was quick to differentiate between spiritual and religious. Religions are based on a set of beliefs about God based on past history and a logical cognitive set of theological ideas. Spirituality is just the opposite – it's based on actual experience in the present moment, focused on intuitive rather than cognitive functions of the mind. Religious beliefs are theological ideas we hope are true; spiritual truths are experiences we know are true – because we've experienced them ourselves. Hopefully, believers in the various world religious traditions experience at least occasional direct encounters with their God, but not necessarily. People who base their lives not on beliefs but on direct experiences of God's presence in their lives tend to be involved in a meditative practice, or naturally inclined to intuitive flashes and spiritual awakening.

Whatever your religious or non-religious stance in life, I'd like to talk with you about the common spiritual experience that people from all cultures and all periods of history have reported having – because these spiritual experiences are entirely congruent with the new scientific research regarding how we can touch other hearts from a distance, make contact spiritually before we do physically, and merge our hearts with like-minded folk simply by sitting quietly and opening our hearts to this experience.

> You might find it valuable right now before we go further into this discussion, to pause and reflect upon whether you consider yourself a religious person, a spiritual person, or a materialist who's confident there are no dimensions beyond the three dimensions that traditional science has identified. Just pause after reading these words, put the book aside, tune into your breathing . . . your heart . . . and look to see if you feel connected with a spiritual dimension of life that exists beyond the reach of your five senses and science's dials and meters . . .

pause . . . breathe . . . reflect . . . experience

Our Collective Unconscious

Although you're probably not aware of it, atmospheric scientists say that with every breath you inhale, chances are high that one or more of the molecules in that air you just inhaled was once also in the lungs and body of Jesus – and also once breathed by Buddha, the Madonna, Lao Tzu, Joan of Arc, John Kennedy and even your great-grandma.

We're all living in the same atmospheric sea – and as the centuries pass, the air in this sea is not being replenished. Sure, it's recycled by the grass, plankton and trees to purify the oxygen of the carbon we breathe out – but the same molecules of oxygen, hydrogen, and other gases that were here before life came into being on this planet, will continue to be breathed to sustain life on this planet . . . for as long as life continues . . .

You are right now breathing the same atmosphere that the lover who is on his or her way into your arms is breathing. You are connected by the air that gives you life. If you were of molecular size, right now you could take off on a trip jumping from one air molecule to the next in the direction of your lover, and end up right at his or her nose – that's how connected you are by the air.

Carl Jung took this scientifically verifiable realization of our atmospheric connection with all other human beings on this planet, and expanded the realization to explain his strange sense of feeling in communion with everyone else at more subtle levels of consciousness. Long before Professor Jahn began proving that there must exist an invisible and as-yet-undiscovered medium surrounding our planet through which our thoughts and intent move and encounter other people's minds and hearts, Professor Jung came up with his concept of the 'collective unconscious' – that invisible shared atmospheric medium into which all our thoughts and feelings are broadcast, which holds these broadcasts and, at times, passes them on to resonant minds and hearts anywhere on the surface of the earth.

The American Indian tradition carries a strong insistence that such an invisible shared medium exists that holds the primal intent and directive, even mood and inclination, of a culture. In the Yaqui tradition this collective unconscious is called the 'tonahl'. Similar understandings are found in the ancient Hindu tradition in India and other religions as well. Christianity and Islam hold the belief (and the experience) that there is an infinite all-knowing spiritual presence that invisibly yet energetically pervades the earthly plane, which all souls can directly tap into and be in communion with.

New studies trying to finally document the presence of human consciousness itself find that in order to make sense of individual consciousness, there must exist a transpersonal consciousness in which we all participate. Indeed within the Buddhist understanding there is without question, based on meditative experience of millions of people, one infinite Conscious Being on this planet, and we are all a conscious part of this greater conscious whole.

Obviously we're still on the path to fully grasping the greater nature of transpersonal consciousness. Meanwhile in virtually all spiritual traditions, individuals have looked within, quieted their busy minds, expanded their awareness to include their hearts – and then expanded their personal bubble of awareness to where they suddenly experienced contact with, and oneness with, a greater consciousness. Buddhists say they have encountered Buddha, Christians encounter Jesus, Moslems merge with Allah, Yaquis commune with Great Spirit.

By whatever name we might want to call it, there is 'something' out there beyond the perimeter of our personal consciousness, of this I also have had considerable experience and know to be a spiritual fact. I am not alone, nor am I separate from the rest of humanity, nor is humanity alone . . . we are all connected, and there exists a greater reality beyond us all, which we label and interpret how we will, but which does exist. My experience, as Buddha and Jesus and all other great spiritual teachers have also taught, is that the primary qualities of this Universal Consciousness can best be described as loving, wise, and powerful – and entirely beyond the confines of space and time.

Do not take my word for any of this. Not even the word of Buddha or Jesus or Allah. After all, wise spiritual teachers say look for yourself – discover God inside your own heart. Come to know the inter-connectedness of all human beings as an experience, not an idea or a belief. Jesus said, 'Know the truth, and the truth will set you free.' He didn't say, believe the dogma, and the dogma will set you free. 'Direct knowledge' in the Greek of the early Bible referred to experience, to conscious encounter, not to ideas and beliefs. I encourage you to likewise seek to know the truth of all this for yourself, through pausing, looking inward, and experiencing the greater consciousness that holds us all together as one world community and family.

Pause if you want to, and after reading this paragraph, close the book and do the following: tune into your breathing . . . experi-ence the air molecules that sustain us all, flowing into your nose and generating a response from your nose's sense receptors . . . fill your lungs with air we are all breathing together . . . feel your connectedness through your breaths as they come . . . and go . . . and come anew . . . and expand your awareness to include the movements in your chest and belly as you breathe . . . and the feelings in your heart right now . . . and as your thoughts become quiet, allow your personal awareness to expand so that you open your heart to feeling one with the world around you . . . connected with all other resonant souls on earth . . . and in communion with the Universal Consciousness that sustains and nurtures and loves us all . . .

pause . . . breathe . . . reflect . . . experience

Help From Above

Many people pray to God for help in finding their true love. Most Christian sects believe that God is actively helping us to find our mate – indeed certain churches believe that there is just one true mate for a person, and that only through God's direction in prayer can this person be found. Even those who have let go of most of our religious tradition in favour of more scientific understandings of causality in the world, tend to hold unconscious assumptions about God being influential in bringing us together with our one true love.

I'm clearly not here to tell you what to believe in this regard, not to take the side of one religion over another in their claim to hold the truth of the matter. Rather we're now exploring various possibilities of what life is all about, so we can expand our concept of mutual attraction wide enough to include certain dimensions that might prove invaluable. I hope you understand that this whole book and process is an exploration, a sharing of experience, and a desire to tap the highest levels possible in our quest for true love.

My direct experience in this regard, for what it's worth, is that there does exist a higher guiding force in my own life. When I surrender and allow that guiding force to influence the thoughts I think, the plans I make, the feelings that come to my heart, and the intent that I project out into the world, my life flows beautifully. When I'm out of touch with that greater guiding force and try to manipulate my life based on my ego's limited vision, my life tends to run amuck and flounder.

Therefore I do my best, each and every moment, to stay aware of my breathing, my heart, and my sense of connectedness with the greater guiding force that permeates human reality. This is where I find my comfort, my strength and my insight – even though at this point in my life I prefer not to adhere to any religious group or theological belief system. What's key for me is staying in communion with God, and doing the work that I'm guided to do.

I say all this because again, I want to give you time to reflect upon your own personal feelings in this regard. See what insights come to you, what feelings come to your heart, when you reflect upon whether the following statements ring true for you when you say them:

'I don't believe at all in any so-called spiritual dimensions to life.'

'There is a loving God who can help direct my life.'

'I myself have experienced that mystic flash of being one with all living beings.'

'I trust God to answer my prayers and bring me my true love.'

'There's no "higher guiding force" – that's just an antiquated superstition.'

'Love is a spiritual presence that permeates and sustains the universe.'

'Love is a biochemical bodily response based on sexual appetite and family bonding.'

'God is love, and I strive to surrender to this higher guiding power in my life.'

'It's pure chance that I'm going to meet somebody who's compatible with me.'

'With higher guidance, I know I'm moving towards meeting my one true love.'

pause . . . breathe . . . reflect . . . experience

Your Mind's Power of Intent

I hope you're enjoying entertaining these various possibilities of how you can maximize your attraction potential. Let's venture into another realm that should prove fruitful, to say the least. You'll remember that I proposed four primary energetic centres in your body that, when activated, balanced and integrated, enable you to generate maximum attraction power as you broadcast into whatever that mysterious connective tissue is between your heart and your lover's heart. Perhaps even in that discussion, your mind said, 'Hey, wait a minute, you're forgetting the most powerful energetic centre I have – my mind!'

True – and I've held discussion of that potent power centre until this chapter only because it will make much more sense in the context of what we're now talking about – consciousness itself, and how we expand consciousness from its centre in our personal brains, outward (or inward) into communion with what we now call transpersonal consciousness, or even Universal Consciousness if we want a spiritual spin. Certainly the human mind remains the primary integrative centre of our personal consciousness, and as such plays a primary role in absolutely everything we do.

Let me share with you my evolving understanding of exactly how the brain does integrate into the other energetic centres of the heart, the genitals, the power centre and the oral centre. When we talk about normal human awareness, we're referring to the composite experience that's generated in our brains, based on inputs from all our senses including our skin, our internal organs, our eyes, ears, nose and mouth. It's important to remember that our brain is not a sense organ, it's the integrative and interpretive centre that takes all the body's sensory inputs, filters out about 99 per cent of the incoming sensory data, and manipulates the remaining data in such a way as to present our conscious awareness with a coherent experience.

We don't ever receive a direct unfiltered sensory experience of the outside world. What we experience is an interpretation of the raw data that matches previous experience, that makes sense based on our beliefs and expectations of what we're experiencing. Often we see what we expect to see, even if it's different from what's really out there. Our minds have the power to take a vague sensory input and fill it in so that it's complete, from previous inputs of a similar nature. In sum, we tend to see what our personality expects to see. Our minds create our experience as much from imagination and expectation, as from the reality we're encountering in the present moment.

This is important to realize because it dramatizes just how important it is to do our homework and advance our own mind's expectations of the true love we seek, if we're to match our imagination with the reality of our new lover. Many people come face to face with a highly compatible person who could indeed prove to be their heart's true desire – but because the sensory input doesn't match the mind's expectation, the chance is forever lost.

Our minds will do their best to come up with a clear image of who we're seeking, and then make plans to go out into the world hunting for this clear image of the ideal lover. The trouble is that by definition we've never encountered this unique person before. So there's no way our minds can put together a composite of past sensory experiences of previous people, and come up with the correct image of the person who will finally fill our arms and hearts.

Beyond The Image

I remember around nine o'clock in the evening that fateful night in Solothurn, hearing the door buzz and walking down the hallway of the house I was staying at in Switzerland. I was alone in the house, and not expecting anyone. For three days I'd been in a most curious state, entirely at peace with myself and at the same time somehow anticipating at any moment the romantic encounter of my life. I opened the door and there stood this dark-haired punky-looking girl quite younger than myself. For years I'd had a basic image in my mind of the woman I was searching for – and this image was just the opposite of the young woman standing on my doorstep in Solothurn.

Yet at deeper levels, in a split second as I looked into this woman's eyes, there was no question (for either of us). It was instant recognition, and even though we at first tried to fight against the recognition because neither of us matched our mind's image of who we were looking for, there was never really any doubt. Our deeper resonance was like wildfire whipping through our hearts – and our minds just had to back off and realize that the actual truth of the matter was very different from the imagined person we'd been expecting.

So as you advance in your preparations for your coming encounter, let's make sure you set yourself as free as possible regarding old images that your mind might be holding, old attitudes and assumptions about the more superficial qualities of your desired mate. We've already explored some of this question in earlier chapters, and will return to the general theme later as well. For now, the more spiritual question is this: who are you going to give primary responsibility for leading your charge up Romance Hill? As you mobilize your power of intent and broadcast out into the world to contact someone out there equally looking for you, are you going to trust your ego attitudes and mental construct of who it is you're seeking? Or are you going to trust most in the higher guidance we've been talking about, where you surrender your sense of ego control, and place your confidence in your more intuitive spiritual dimensions of awareness?

And here we arrive at a most fascinating and empowering point in our discussion – because when you practise the attraction meditation I'm in the process of presenting and teaching to you, you're actually step by step leading yourself through your ego directives and cognitive levels of intent, to the point where you expand your awareness to include your higher powers of guidance and manifestation.

Note that first of all I have you turn your attention to your breathing in a special way that, in and of itself, actually serves to quiet the flow of thoughts through your mind. Those of you who have read some of my earlier books know this 'quiet mind' technique already. Psychologically when you focus on two or more sensory inputs at the same time (the air flowing in and out your nose + the sensations of movement in your chest and belly as you breathe, for instance) your mind lets go of linear thinking and logic quite naturally, and shifts into a more intuitive 'seeing all at once' state of mind. And this expansion of consciousness to being aware of your whole body at once leads you right to the point where you do encounter your higher self, your deeper intuitive soul, and your transpersonal encounter with whatever you want to call God's guiding wisdom and love.

I often return to the basic spiritual saying that is found in all the world's great religious traditions: 'Not my will, but thine, O God.' Psychologically this statement represents the surrender of the usual ego-thinking mind to the greater intuitive spiritual mind – and my experience is that people have a vastly greater chance of finding true love when they surrender to their greater intuitive guide and stop trying to 'make romance happen'. This is why I've called this book 'Let Love Find You', because as long as your ego mind thinks it's going to force the world to present your ideal lover, not much is going to happen. The ego is smart, but it's not wise. The thinking mind can reflect on past personal experience and come up with a composite image of your ideal lover, but it can't expand in the present moment and come directly into encounter with the actual person out there who is searching equally for you – only the greater transpersonal consciousness that transcends personal limitations can do that.

So call it what you will – I encourage you to explore your own capacity to go transpersonal in your search for your beloved. Yes, it's important to do the homework I've laid out for you in previous chapters of healing old heart wounds, identifying negative attitudes, and getting clear in your logical thinking mind your basic goal and the process that will most accelerate your movement towards your lover. But also, regularly explore the dimensions of the attraction meditations you're learning here, that will enable you to surrender to your higher guide, and allow that deep inner guidance to intuitively move you closer and closer to contact!

Let's see what happens when you simply do what we've been talking about. Even if you don't necessarily believe much of what I've been talking about in this chapter, the scientific approach here is to do the experiment a number of times, and experience for yourself the truth of the matter. When you open your mind, heart and soul to a greater consciousness, when you look openly and honestly in the direction of a loving transpersonal presence and guidance in your life – what do you find?

We could of course talk for hours on this topic because we have our finger here on the very pulse of human experience itself. You'll find plenty of discussion in this direction at my website if you want more. For now, let's turn our attention towards your own experience here in this present moment. Talk-about is never as important as look-and-listen. What really does happen inside your own mind when you do a simple perceptual meditation that effectively, if at least for a short while, helps quiet your usual flow of thoughts, and points your mind's attention directly towards your greater awareness that comes into being when your ego mind surrenders the stage for a while? We'll start with the basic focusing meditation you've been learning, and then expand in new directions . . .

Exercise Six: TAPPING YOUR HIGHER ATTRACTION POWER

Make sure you're comfortable . . . stretch a bit if you want . . . yawn all you want to . . . and gently allow your eyes to close when they want to . . . tune into your breathing . . . the air flowing in your nose, and out, and in again . . . and at the same time, expand your awareness to include the movements in your chest and belly as you breathe . . . make no effort to breathe . . . let your breathing stop when it wants to . . . be empty of air . . . and let your breathing start again when it wants to . . . set your breathing free . . .

As you stay aware of your breathing, allow your awareness to expand to also include the feelings in your heart, right in the middle of your breathing . . . accept what you find in your heart . . . say to yourself, '*I love myself, just as I am* . . .' and breathe into the feeling of acceptance, and love.

As you stay aware of your breathing, and your heart, let your awareness expand to include your whole body, here in this present moment . . . your breathing . . . your heart . . . your feet . . . your fingers . . . your tongue . . . your knees . . . your head . . . your whole body right now . . . and say to yourself, *'My heart is open to receive, God's healing love . . .'* (or whatever equivalent you feel comfortable with) and breathe into this wonderful feeling of opening your heart, and letting the love come flowing in . . .

As the love flows in and fills your heart, allow your awareness to expand beyond your personal body, to include the air around you . . . let yourself be aware of all the like-minded people in the world breathing this same air . . . all of you opening your hearts to love . . . all of you tuning into your spiritual source that guides you and sustains you . . . and say to yourself, *'I feel connected with my source . . .'*

As you continue to feel connected with your guiding light, one with your higher self, you can also now expand your awareness to tune into the person out there in the world who some day will suddenly be standing in front of you, looking into your eyes – and recognizing you as you recognize them . . . and say, *'I feel you . . . I love you . . . I'm waiting for you!'*

And when you're ready, you can just relax . . . feel your breaths coming and going . . . and while you stay tuned in and connected heart to heart with your lover, you can open your eyes whenever you want . . . stretch and yawn if that feels good . . . and go on with your day – knowing in your heart that you are not alone . . . that you are one with your spiritual creator . . . and one with your true love . . .

pause . . . breathe . . . reflect . . . experience

Chapter 7

Focus...
Broadcast...
Contact...
Encounter

HEART ENCOUNTER – SEVEN

Nicolas and Angie had known each other all through school but they preferred to mostly ignore each other – because both of them were quite chubby but didn't want to associate with other chubbies. It wasn't fun being fat and both of them had found niches at school where how they looked wasn't as important as what they could do. Nicolas was the funny guy, and he could draw cartoons of anyone he wanted to – so he was in the in crowd even though he wasn't a handsome guy – he could keep his friends laughing. Meanwhile Angie was the serious girl who got her first short story published when she was fifteen. It was a year later that their mutual fate exploded, and here's how Nicolas remembers it:

I suppose my life was okay because people liked me and invited me to parties because of my drawings and jokes, but on the other hand, none of the girls I was interested in ever showed any interest in me at all, as far as sex was concerned. I was just the fat kid who made people laugh, and right around when I turned sixteen I started getting really depressed. I tried dieting like crazy to lose weight, but I just couldn't stop myself from gobbling, I had this hunger way deep inside me, who knows why, maybe because my mom had died when I was just little – I was tired of all the analysis, the truth was, I felt lonely as hell and I ate all the time.

Yeah, I knew Angie, we'd known each other for loads of years, she was the other fat kid in class. And then she was shifted over to a different class so I didn't talk to her much, I just saw her waddling along the corridors and seeing her made me cringe at how I myself must look, so I'd look anywhere but at Angie. Oh, I read her short story and it was real good, but I don't think I ever complimented her. I was starting to do more serious drawing now, portraits of people. I'd even gotten paid a few times, and I was only sixteen, so that made me feel good. But I was alone a lot, my buddies mostly had girlfriends and weren't hanging out so much with me, and it just got more and more depressing. I'd dream of some beautiful girl falling in love with fat ol' me and having a totally wild sexual time with her – but that was just dreams.

One day I got halfway home and then remembered I'd forgotten a book from the school library that I needed for homework, so I had to trudge all the way back up the hill in the heat. Walking into the cool library was great, my mood seemed to shift upwards suddenly. Rather than feeling in a hurry, I was feeling something else – comfortable right where I was. I sat down with the book and read some of it in the cool of the reading room. Time passed. I stared off into space a bit, envisioning a new drawing I was going to start that afternoon.

Suddenly the idea popped into my mind of going over to the media room and checking out something on the web, and I hopped up without any more thoughts and walked down the hall and into the room, which was luckily still open with the media instructor talking to a student. When I saw who the student was I habitually reacted – Angie. She had her back to me, and was standing with most of her weight on one foot, in a posture that was somehow intriguing. Just like that, as was my custom, I pulled out my sketch book and started doing a quick sketch of her. Then she shifted weight and I sketched that position. The curious thing was, even though she was chubby, there was a lot of grace in her lines, and the way she shifted her hips back and forth seemed somehow sexy – she was obviously alive inside her body, probably more than I was.

She turned around as if sensing me fifteen feet away drawing her.

'What are you doing?' she accused me.

'Nothing – just drawing you. Is that a crime?'

'Possibly,' she said right back at me – and then came over and grabbed my sketch pad out of my hands. She stood there looking at what I'd drawn, her expression shifting from angry to confused and then – well, she blushed.

'What are you doing, trying to turn me into a sex object?' she accused again.

'Only if you are one,' I said hotly back to her.

'Well I'm as sexy as anybody else but that's not how I look.'

'Want to bet?'

The media instructor came over and took a look. 'Oh, that's really quite good – and sure, that's how you look, at least from Nicolas's eyes,' he said. 'You can look as sexy as you want to.'

'Sure, fat and sexy,' she said, mocking herself.

'Why not?' the instructor told her. 'Two hundred years ago skinny girls were considered ugly and chubby girls beautiful, you know that.'

'Well give me the time-travel machine, I'm out of here,' she joked.

'I'm coming with you,' I said impulsively.

She turned and looked right at me a moment. The instructor walked off to his desk. She looked back at the drawing. She didn't say anything.

'You can have it if you want,' I offered.

'The last thing I want are pictures of me.'

'You look good there.'

'But I don't look good to anyone else,' she admitted.

'So – join the club.'

'You don't look so bad,' she told me.

'I was on this diet last month and I thought I was going to die.'

She laughed. I'm not sure I'd ever heard her laugh, at least not that light lilting laugh that seemed to rise up from deep inside her. 'I'll match you stories on diet horrors any day.'

'So maybe that's just you,' I said, again looking down at her, and realizing that she had beautiful breasts – then looking back up into her eyes. 'I've got to the place where what you see is what you get, this is me, I can't change it.'

She eyed me a long moment. 'Nicolas, I wouldn't want you to change yourself one iota. I've always liked you – you've just always ignored me.'

I didn't have anything to say to that, I looked away; the media instructor was watching us, interested – he looked quickly back to his computer screen.

'I've just finished a story,' she was saying. 'About being fat.'

'Oh great.'

'Damn you, Nicolas! Stop it!'

'Stop what?'

'You're one of those people who's prejudiced against your own kind.'

'Maybe you are too. So what is your story about?'

'Want to read it?' she offered shyly.

'Uhm – sure.'

She pulled out a copy of the short story and handed it to me – and turned around just like that, and walked out of the room.

That evening instead of drawing, I read her story. It was fairly long and it was really sort of embarrassing to read because she was being more honest than I could ever be, about her feelings of being fat. And then she was talking about her sex feelings and that was double embarrassing – but exciting at the same time. I'd never somehow thought of Angie as feeling sexy but there she was, with her fat character at school thinking all sorts of sex things about the other kids in class – and then her fat girl hero sees a fat boy in the class . . . and starts watching him, and wondering if he's feeling all sorts of sexy feelings under his blubber just like she is.

Well the story was a bother to read – and when I happened to run into Angie a couple of days later I was still embarrassed to talk to her but she hurried down the corridor and, right in front of a bunch of people, pulled me to a stop.

'You read the story?' she asked me.

'Uhm – yeah.'

'So be honest, what did you think – I haven't shown it to anyone else yet.'

'Do we have to talk about this here?'

'I'm late anyway – after school, at the fountain.'

She turned and walked away – she seemed to be good at exits, and she sure was a lot more pushy than I'd expected. But I went to the fountain after school and she was standing there talking to somebody, a boy – and all of a sudden I felt jealous that she was standing close to some other guy talking to him like that. I stopped and almost walked away, but again her posture caught my eye, and all of a sudden I was seeing just how sexy she was, even though she was entirely out of the current beauty mode of our times – still she somehow turned me on, I couldn't take my eyes off her. So I sat down and took out my pad and started drawing her again, getting lost in my excitement of discovering exactly what curves she was made of, and realizing that yeah, I liked how she looked even though she looked, well – no better than I did in the eyes of the masses.

Suddenly she was walking over towards me and I closed my drawing pad. She sat down beside me on the bench.

'Come on, let me see,' she said.

'But these aren't –'

She grabbed the pad from me, not aggressively – and I kind of liked her acting the way she was, being so interested. But when she saw the drawings she tensed.

'My God, how dare you – I'm naked!' she said.

'Yeah, well, actually these are just some drawings of that girl in your story, and you had her stark naked and doing all sorts of naked things,' I retorted. 'Besides, hey, you look good naked.'

She was ready to shout at me – but then something happened and she just continued looking into my eyes for the longest time. Then she said in a mere whisper. 'Do you – do you really think so?'

I shrugged my shoulders. 'There's the proof,' I said, pointing to a particularly sexy picture of her as I imagined she'd look with her clothes off.

A whole bunch of feelings rushed across her expression and before I knew it, she was beaming with the most beautiful smile, her lips so beautiful – and then she was leaning right towards me and kissing me on the lips in front of everybody. 'I can't believe this,' she said – and jumped up and hurried away.

I sat for half an hour that night by the phone with her number at the tip of my fingers, the idea of her naked making me so shaky that I couldn't phone her. When the phone rang I jumped – and before I even picked it up, I knew it would be her . . .

We have arrived at the seventh step, the seventh tone in our attraction scale . . . and are ready to talk a bit about that distance you'll be travelling after you feel connected with your approaching new love, and the moment of encounter. At the beginning of each chapter I've been recounting some of the many encounter stories people have told me about their own experiences of finding each other. I'm looking forward to posting your own story as well on the web, if you'll share it with me, once your coming together is history.

For now, you're just beginning to have a concrete feel for the seven-step daily attraction meditation that I'm teaching here. Towards the end of this chapter I'd like to review what we've learned, and give you a solid outline of each of the steps of the meditation. Then in the next chapter we'll move into action gear with Part Two, 'Manifesting The Desired Encounter'.

As you've seen from the mostly random assortment of encounter memoirs that I've posted at the beginning of these first seven chapters, no matter what we might do for preparation, and no matter how ready we might feel for love, the actual moment of encounter is always going to be both thrilling, exciting, and at least a bit scary. We hunger so intensely for that moment of encounter, but most of us are at least somewhat afraid of it. Let's deal with this apprehension dimension of love at first sight now rather than later.

Here you are right now, living without a lover – and only in your dreams and imagination plunging into the wild unbridled intimacies of sexual relating. You're surely not alone if you feel anxious and uncertain, to say nothing of downright panicked, at the reality of skin-to-skin encounter you're asking for. We're all at least somewhat bashful when it comes to taking our clothes off and actually 'doing it' and 'going all the way' with someone, especially with a new lover who thrills us with the deep but tenuous hope of long-term involvement and happiness.

A great many people actually sabotage their potential moments of encounter because when it comes right down to it, they're afraid of the shock and embarrassment and emotional nakedness that is liable to accompany the experience of meeting someone, looking in their eyes, and getting hit with the jolt of romantic recognition. Are you one of these people? Let's find out. See how you would respond – *yes* or *no* or *sometimes* – to the following statements:

ONE: When I think about suddenly meeting my new lover, I feel shaky and afraid.

TWO: I'm not at all afraid to finally come face to face with my true love.

THREE: I avoid situations where I might encounter a stranger who is attracted to me.

FOUR: When I finally meet my new love, I'm afraid I'm going to choke up and act stupid.

FIVE: I'm very shy about someone feeling sexually attracted to me – and showing it.

SIX: I have an approach-avoidance problem with actively seeking out my new lover.

SEVEN: I'm afraid of being overwhelmed or embarrassed when true love strikes.

We're going to focus on several different dimensions of 'encounter-phobia' in the next few chapters, so don't feel bad if you're like most people and apprehensive about the very thing you're craving – finally coming face to face and heart to heart with that special person you've been feeling in your heart and communing with from a distance. The good news is that through proper preparation of your heart and emotions and expectations before you meet, you'll be quite ready to experience love at first sight without undue trauma.

One of the curious qualities of romantic encounter as my colleagues and I have observed from hundreds, even thousands of case studies, is that for most people the moment of encounter is quite unexpected. You will tend to be minding your own business just before the encounter, in a special state of awareness that, as we'll see in detail, is both actively aware and looking for that flash of eye contact, and at the same time inwardly content and happy inside your own skin to the point where you feel no time pressure because you're already balanced and satisfied on your own.

In this state of mind and emotion, you go about your days and weeks and perhaps even months enjoying life and also ready to find what you're looking for. And then you turn a corner, you open a door, you look up, you hear a voice – and as if time suddenly stands still and the universe pauses for breath, you experience a flash of recognition, a lurching of your heart as it actually feels the closeness of a heart resonating in synch with yours . . . and right at that moment, you enter a perfect world where all your anticipations mean nothing, where all your preparation falls away, and the uniqueness of the moment takes your breath away – and then brings new life into your lungs and heart and soul . . .

Let's pause before we go further here, and give you time to put the book away if you want, and tune into your breathing . . . notice how you feel in your heart as a result of what we've been talking about – how do you feel about the anticipation of the romantic encounter that's coming closer and closer to happening in your life, each new day you practise your attraction meditations and employ your power of intent to encourage this encounter – look and see how you feel right now:

pause . . . breathe . . . reflect . . . experience

Ready For Love

As I've mentioned before, far too many people push themselves into relationships before they're ready for what they're asking for. Yes, it's true that no one can foretell when lightning will strike. Perhaps the love of your life will burst into your intimate world before you can hardly even begin to prepare. If so, of course you just do your best, and still spend time with the early steps of this attraction programme where you make sure you've healed from early romantic wounds. But in most cases, if we're not ready for true love, the sexual partners who we might take to bed aren't likely to remain there overlong.

I know all too well the deep aching pain of a heart that's lonely and yearning for companionship and total oneness with a true lover. But I also know all too well the added agony of grabbing at the first possible lover who comes by – and having to add the pain of that failed romance to all the rest of the heartache already accumulated. All I can say is this: do your best to focus inward and prepare your heart for love, before reaching out overmuch and surrendering your heart into the embrace of the first open arms to appear.

Check out the following 'Ready To Love' list – and remember that the lists I present are special in that each sentence is designed not just to communicate information, but to awaken within you a host of associated feelings and thoughts to help you to explore your feelings.

Process is everything. Inner experience and insight is golden. And only when you take time and look within, using focus phrases to stimulate inner reflection, do you put yourself in position to have a new experience.

So do be sure, before you approach a list of statements like the one below, that you remember the magic trick for turning up your experience burner – make sure you're aware of the air flowing in and out your nose or mouth . . . expand to be aware of the movements in your chest and belly as you breathe . . . expand to be aware of the feelings in your heart right now . . . be aware of your whole body, here in this present moment . . . and in this expanded alert state of whole-body awareness, read and breathe into each statement, and allow the words to awaken feelings, insights and new experience within you – in this instance, related to the question of whether you're really ready for the flash of encounter you yearn for. And rather than just going through this list once, return to it once a week or so, to see how you're progressing:

READY TO LOVE: The List

ONE: Are you fully recovered from your past love relationships, so that you're no longer painfully caught up emotionally in the collapse of that old romance?

TWO: Have you forgiven all your old lovers, and let go of blaming others for what they did to you, and feeling guilty for your own actions or inactions?

THREE: Have you chosen to be your own best friend, and reached the point where you no longer feel needy and grasping for another person's acceptance and love?

FOUR: Have you mastered the fine art of loving yourself just as you are, and opening your heart regularly to the inflow of love into your heart?

FIVE: Can you be with yourself alone, tune into your breathing and your feelings, and enjoy the company of your own presence without feeling lonely?

SIX: Have you learned how to experience your own body, and awaken pleasure throughout your physical being?

SEVEN: Can you quiet your thoughts and tune into your own heart, and open up to feel the presence of all the people out there in the world who resonate with a similar yearning and intent as you do?

EIGHT: Do you feel that you have made heart contact with your true love who is out there also yearning for you – are you open to receive contact and love from this person even before you meet?

NINE: When you tune into your new lover out there somewhere, and look to your own heart, do you feel ready to be with this person physically? Are you ready to shift into active hunting mode, to manifest your lover?

TEN: Can you readily imagine turning a corner, seeing your true love in front of you suddenly, and walking up and just opening your arms to embrace them . . . are you ready to touch and to hold and to caress your true new love?

pause . . . breathe . . . reflect . . . experience

Synchronicity In Abundance

The truly great Swiss psychoanalyst Carl Jung created a new word to express a universal phenomenon he considered one of the most important ingredients of human life – synchronicity. Rather than accepting the common Newtonian scientific notion that life operates on random chance, he insisted on pointing out that for him, life is full of 'chance happenings' that are anything but random. As we mentioned before, Jung observed that if two people are going to turn a corner and run into each other two days from now, then right now they are on a collision course with each other. Their movements are synchronized in advance, in order for them to be at the same time at the same place sometime in the future. Einstein and others developed this new sense of 'chance occurrence' further with their expansion of our concept of time itself so that the present moment is somehow 'warped' in space to touch the past and the future.

Time is perhaps the most mysterious ingredient in this experience we call consciousness. Here you are right now in this present moment, located exactly at a certain grid in space and time. And somewhere in the distance away from you is the person you're going to run into and meet at some future date, and fall in love with. If you leap ahead to the moment of encounter, and then run both of your lives backwards in time to right now, you will see as Jung pointed out that there were thousands, even millions of little decisions you made in your life that enabled both of you to end up at the same time at the same place for your fated encounter.

Synchronicity is that seemingly magical sense of attunement that two separate people enter into in this present moment, where they remain connected with each other so that with each decision each of them makes, they move towards that fated encounter with each other. Jung admitted that science still doesn't know the dynamics of this synchronicity – but he surely had experienced it enough in his own life to know that it exists. I suspect you know too from personal experience. Life is more than just random happenings. Life seems to have a greater integrity that transcends linear time and physical space, and links like-minded folk together at deeper heart levels.

All I'm doing is helping you tune into this synchronous dimension of life, so that you too can actively make heart contact with someone in synch with you out there . . . and step by step, allow each and every decision you make to guide you and this person towards your coming encounter. I know of many couples who actually passed each other by ten, twenty times as they both went to work in similar patterns but missed each other – until they were ready for the encounter. Then it happened – bam!

And meanwhile other couples, like my wife and I, started out so distant and in such different movement patterns that the chances were utterly impossible for us to find each other, except for the synchronicity factor where for weeks in advance, each of us made choices that changed our movement patterns to where suddenly we were congruent in space and time – and blessed with the encounter we were both feeling entirely ready for.

We're talking about something so serious it's important not to get too serious! Yes, there is some great mysterious force that is pulling you and your new lover together – but at the same time, this force is not so mysterious or unusual because you are actually always immersed in the power of love to guide you. You are always being touched by God's guiding hand in your decisions and actions. This magical thing called romantic encounter is utterly natural and normal. The challenge is simply to surrender your life to this transpersonal force, and relax as you enter into the certainty that love is coming your way, at its own good time, when you're more than ready.

And luckily, the preparation path you're now learning to walk is utterly enjoyable in and of itself, so you can enjoy every moment along the way towards your true love – and thus maximize your success in preparing your heart fully for your lover. Pause and breathe into this most wonderful present moment right now that we're sharing . . . see how your heart feels . . . accept . . . enjoy!

pause . . . breathe . . . reflect . . . experience

The Seven Steps Together

I've now taught you the basic ingredients of the seven steps in the daily attraction meditation that I'm encouraging you to soon make time and space for in your everyday routine, once or even twice a day. When you get to the end of this book, I hope you'll go back and re-read these first seven chapters so that you truly master each step.

To end this first part of the book, I'd like to give you a short experience of each of the seven steps in the attraction meditation, so that in a short space you understand the fullness of the programme – then in the next chapter I'll show you how to actively bring this daily practice into your life, in several variations depending on your available time and preferences.

Each of these seven steps, even though there's loads of potent content and room for insight and growth in each, can actually be compressed into four primary focus phrases – which you have already read once. The magic of these phrases, as I've said before, is that when you say them to yourself in a reflective state of mind, they carry the associative power to resonate deep within your mind and soul. As you pause and breathe into the impact of the words on your inner world, they will almost magically awaken new insights, emotional healing, and attraction power.

Sometimes you'll simply (yet importantly) experience nothing more than a slight shift in how you feel in your heart – this subtle change of feelings in your heart is primary because over a period of a few days or a week, you'll find that your heart has indeed changed, expanded, opened up and received the healing and insight and power you're asking for.

Sometimes you'll say one of these sentences, close your eyes and breathe into its impact – and be touched by a flash of insight, a meaningful memory, or a strong inflow of love and energy to move you effortlessly in the direction you desire. Three phrases per step, times seven steps, equals twenty-one stimulants lined up in a very special order, to guide you daily through the entire inner process that encourages emotional healing, clarification of intent, and the actual heart-to-heart communion and mutual attraction that you're yearning to experience.

Exercise Seven: THE ATTRACTION MEDITATION
You can employ this attraction meditation each day to direct your mind's attention exactly where it needs to focus. These simple powerful statements are mind-management tools for activating your natural

capacity to attract fulfilling love into your life – and you can move through this process in just ten minutes or so.

Tune into your breathing . . . and read the first focus phrase . . . for a few breaths you can close your eyes, say the sentence again to yourself – and be open to whatever new experience emerges effortlessly as the words resonate deep within you . . . awakening new feelings and insights . . . relax . . . open up . . . experience. . .

1. Yearning
'I want to heal my emotional wounds . . .'
'I feel a deep yearning for new love . . .'
'I am going to attract new love to me . . .'

2. Forgiving and Healing
'I accept and love myself, just as I am.'
'I forgive and let go of my old lovers.'
'My heart is open to receive . . . healing . . . and love.'

3. Waking Up Sexually
'I am a beautiful powerful sexual being.'
'I give myself permission to feel good in my body.'
'See me – sexually attractive . . . ready for love.'

4. Charging
'I feel passion . . . in my heart . . . in my belly . . .'
'I feel sexual hunger in my genitals . . . in my throat . . .'
'My whole being is charged with loving energy.'

5. Broadcasting
'Here I am right now, yearning for love.'
'I am reaching out to you . . .'
'Feel me . . . come into my life.'

6. Surrendering
'My mind is quiet . . . my breathing calm.'
'I request help from my deeper source.'
'I surrender to spiritual wisdom and guidance.'

7. Moving Towards Encounter
'I let go of inhibitions . . .'
'I need you . . . I love you . . .'
'Here I am – I feel you!'

pause . . . breathe . . . reflect . . . experience

Part Two

MANIFESTING THE DESIRED ENCOUNTER

Chapter 8

Attraction –
In Action

N ow that you have a basic feeling for the actual process of the attraction-meditation discussion, it's time to get enjoyably pragmatic as we focus now on your current personal situation, explore the next steps you're set to make towards finding your true love, and begin practising the daily meditation in a format that fits your time-frame and personal lifestyle. It's one thing to read about a powerful mind-management technique like this one. It's an entirely different matter to move beyond 'thinking about' doing something in the future, and actually shift into action mode, and do it in this present moment – on a regular basis and progressing until you reach your ultimate goal.

In this chapter I'm going to teach you three formats for our general attraction-meditation theme. You can decide for yourself which format you want to activate in your daily life – meaning right now, today, and tomorrow, and the day after that . . . forward right through your preparation and encounter, your first wild days and nights and right on into what hopefully will prove to be a long-term, ultimately fulfilling relationship.

In the next chapter we'll talk about the actual process you're going to shift into when you feel ready, of actively hunting for your true love. The attraction meditation will move mountains in many ways towards preparing your heart and bringing you into heart contact with your lover. But ultimately by the laws of physical encounter you're going to need to start moving around this planet upon which your new lover is also moving, such that you open up ample opportunity to be guided into physical congruence with the person you desire. I call this the romantic hunt, and I assure you, you'll have great fun on this hunt, once you're prepared for it!

In chapter ten we'll discuss a very special dimension to the romantic hunt – the fine art of remaining unattached to the outcome of your hunt. You'll at first perhaps think it's a paradox that you must both strongly intend to find your true love, and at the same time act as if you don't care if you do or not. But trust me, this 'nonattachment to outcomes' attitude is the final step in totally activating your attraction power. The more needy you are, the less powerful you'll be in hunt mode. Only when you are entirely open to never finding your true love, do you attain optimum power to manifest your desired encounter. This aspect of the romantic hunt reflects one of the deepest aspects of the spiritual meditative path in general – that you can't push to make love come to you, all you can do is relax, surrender, and allow love to come to you.

Chapter eleven is devoted to preparing you at several dimensions to handle the excitement that develops on the romantic hunt, so that this excitement doesn't throw off your keenness of observation and readiness for the encounter. The general emotion of excitement needs to be examined closely here, because excitement usually carries a lot of apprehension and even anxiety at its centre – and we need to reduce the apprehension if we're to amp up the sense of expanding desire and readiness that also fuels your excitement.

And then we come to chapter twelve where indeed, it happens – the desired encounter in the future becomes a present-moment event. How will you respond to this actual face-to-face experience? We'll look closely at several aspects of the encounter experience, and let you prepare for the encounter so that you make sure it's a success.

Doing It

Each moment that you spend consciously turning your romantic desires and yearnings into active attraction energy, you're moving closer towards your new lover. Each moment you spend focused in your heart and whole body, broadcasting your presence and love out into the world towards like-minded folk who're also broadcasting towards you, you're increasing your power of synchronicity with the person you're destined to meet. When you have half an hour to pause and move through the full attraction meditation, that's wonderful. And when you have just a minute or two, you can do a shortened version of the attraction meditation so that you consciously reach out to your lover more often than just once a day. In fact, as we'll see in this chapter, you can actively reach out many many times a day – and why not!

In a great many important ways, the more often each day that you turn your attention towards your heart and whole-body presence, the better your life is going to progress. The more you're aware of your breathing experience, in all that you do, the more conscious and alive you're going to be. I think you're aware by now that the programme I'm teaching you isn't just for romantic success, it's a general process for brightening your spirit, healing your emotional wounds, staying connected with your creative source, and making sure that your heart is full of love – for everyone you relate with each new day.

So I encourage you to establish the intent of taking just a minute or two, ten or twenty or even thirty times a day, to pause and let go your habitual worries and problem-solving thoughts, so you can turn your attention to your core of experiential life, and awaken your deeper sense of who you are in this eternal present moment. This is not at all an esoteric notion, this is a very pragmatic approach to optimizing your success at work, your reduced-stress health profile, your popularity in your social group, and your general creative clarity and expression.

So let's learn a very short heart-awakening process, a three to four minute deeper attraction meditation, and of course, the full-length half-hour daily or twice-daily meditation. My role isn't to insist that you do these meditations regularly, that's your responsibility entirely. I'm here to offer you the path, and encourage you to walk it towards your desired heart goal. You're the one in the end who taps your romantic yearning energy, and uses it to get what you want – through meditation in action.

You might want to pause a moment, to tune into your breathing . . . your heart . . . your whole-body presence . . . and reflect upon your present intent to actually set aside time each day to do the attraction meditation. Are you wanting to pause at least a few times each day wherever you might be, to spend a few minutes and tune into your heart's desires and broadcast your desire out to your lover? And are you also wanting to set aside a formal half-hour at some point in each day as a devoted ritual, where you purposefully move through the full attraction meditation and actively attract your lover?

pause . . . breathe . . . reflect . . . experience

Short-Short Heart Awakening

In just one minute, you can pause (without people around you even knowing you're doing it) and awaken your heart to the inflow of love, and the wonderful feeling of being connected heart-to-heart with your approaching lover. Once you practise this and get good at it, you'll find it feels so good that you do it more and more – which will genuinely transform your life in positive directions:

The first step in this short-short heart meditation is remembering the process, and your desire to do it regularly. I recommend you go around for the next few days saying the focus phrase 'short short' to yourself over and over . . . short short . . . short short . . . so that the basic concept becomes imbedded in your mind.

- And each time you say to yourself, 'short short' all you need to do is to remember to turn your mind's attention to your breathing. You breathe around six times a minute. On the first breath, say, 'nose' and feel the air flowing in and out your nose . . .
- On your second breath, say 'chest' and feel the sensation of the air rushing in and out your nose or mouth, and also the sensations of movement in your chest and belly as you breathe.
- On your third breath, say the word 'heart' to yourself, and let this powerful pointer word expand your awareness to include the feelings in your heart . . .
- On your fourth breath, hold the word 'open' in your mind . . . and experience the wonderful feeling of love flowing into your heart, just through remembering to pause and open up your heart . . .
- On your fifth breath, say to your lover who is also seeking you, 'Here I am . . .' Enjoy the feeling of being connected already in your heart, with your yet-to-be-found lover. And broadcast your love and your presence outward strongly, riding on the winds of your heart's desire.
- And on your sixth breath, just allow your mind to be quiet as your breathing continues, and you enjoy the warm loving feeling in your heart of being in communion both with the universal love of God and humanity, and also the specific love of the person you're in deepest heart contact with . . .

And there you have it – six breaths that awaken your heart, make contact with the love that permeates the universe, and broadcast your presence and love outward to your approaching lover . . . one minute of your day. One minute to pause and make yourself feel better in your heart, to encourage your breathing to relax and deepen, to connect with your deeper spiritual presence, and also connect with the person you're attracting to you, each time you pause for this short-short attraction meditation. Here is the six-breath one-minute attraction meditation at a glance to memorize:

BREATH ONE: Pause and remember you want to do the short-short meditation.

BREATH TWO: Turn your mind's full attention to your breathing experience.

BREATH THREE: Expand your awareness to include the feelings in your heart.

BREATH FOUR: Open your heart to receive . . . love.

BREATH FIVE: Say to yourself, *'Here I am!'*

BREATH SIX: Enjoy the good feelings of love and connection in your heart and body.

Four-Minute Attraction

You can do the one-minute short-short meditation virtually anywhere, and I encourage you to do it at least once an hour – or more! And here's a four-minute meditation that can also be done almost anywhere, except that you'll need a slightly longer space of undisturbed time, which shouldn't be hard to find if you truly desire it – maybe four to six times a day. I know of corporations that actually encourage their employees to take a five-minute meditation breather each hour, because to do so is beneficial on all fronts.

In this somewhat expanded attraction meditation, we're going to again employ key focus phrases (drawn from the full attraction meditation) to instantly turn your mind's attention in powerful rewarding directions. And I repeat yet again: each time you say one of these focus phrases and turn your mind's attention towards the vast realm of experiences and associations the phrase elicits, you're going to have a new experience. This psychological process is so powerful because the more you do it, the deeper you go, as you progress step by step into unknown realms of your own being, and awaken feelings and insights that reflect the just-emerging newness of your own heart and soul.

So don't be fooled by the seeming simplicity of a programme based on just a few sentences – I've compressed the programme down to these key focus phrases with the specific intent of making the programme easy for you to memorize and move through on your own. Feel free during your learning process to go online at www.johnselby.com and listen to me guiding you through the meditations, or get the CD so you can listen to the audio guidance anywhere. But hold in mind that our intent is for you to memorize the process so that wherever you are, you can guide yourself effortlessly through the meditations – simply by remembering a few focus phrases.

This four-minute attraction meditation is based on seven focus phrases. You simply memorize them one way or the other, and remember to pause for four minutes – and after tuning into your breathing and heart presence, say each of these phrases one after the other, pausing for two or three breaths to reflect and experience . . .

First of course you'll need to remember to pause . . . and give yourself about five minutes free of distractions. You can do this meditation while commuting to work each day (yes, you can do it while driving!), or pause at work when you're free for a short break. You can go for a short walk and move through the focus phrases while walking, or riding your bike – or while sitting quietly somewhere in nature. You can effortlessly settle into your favourite chair at home, or lie down on the rug, or bed. You can have your eyes open (if driving!) or closed.

Begin the meditation by moving through the usual beginning process of turning your mind's attention to your breaths coming and going through your nose or mouth . . . expand your awareness to include the movements in your chest and belly as you breathe without any effort . . . expand your awareness to include the feelings you find in your heart . . . and expand another step to be aware of your whole body, here in this present moment . . .

In this expanded state of awareness, where your thoughts have become naturally quiet, say the following seven focus phrases to yourself, pausing after each one for a few breaths to open up to new experience – and then move on to the next:

ONE: *'I feel my desire for new love.'*

TWO: *'I forgive all my old lovers.'*

THREE: *'I accept and love myself, just as I am.'*

FOUR: *'My heart is open to receive.'*

FIVE: *'I am a beautiful powerful sexual being.'*

SIX: *'I surrender to the greater power guiding me.'*

SEVEN: *'I love you . . . I need you . . . here I am!'*

To help you memorize these seven focus phrases, in the back of this book you'll find each meditation printed, one per page, for fast reference. You can also Xerox the meditation if you want to, or as mentioned before, go online and let me lead you through the meditation a few times, until you memorize it by heart. After a while you'll become so familiar with the process that you'll hardly need to say the next phrase before your mind naturally moves on to the next dimension of the meditation.

I recommend that you pause here, and go back and actually do the four-minute meditation now, so that it begins to take root in your soul . . .

pause . . . breathe . . . reflect . . . experience

Daily Meditation – Finding Time

Have you ever before set aside a particular time each day, to do something special – such as practise a musical instrument, or play an athletic sport, or perhaps move through a traditional meditation process? There's something very wonderful that comes into being when you say to the world, 'Regardless of what else is happening in the world, each day of my life I personally pause for half an hour, in order to nurture what I consider most important to me. Please respect this special time that I have set aside for my own growth and enjoyment.'

As you now approach the possibility of setting aside half an hour or so (actually you can spend fifteen minutes to forty-five minutes depending on the pace you move through the focus phrases), how are you feeling about this prospect? Can you make time in your busy schedule for this important new activity? Do you want to? And practically, how are you going to manage your daily schedule to create time for your daily attraction meditation?

I assure you that if you don't almost forcefully insist on changing your schedule to include your attraction meditation, you won't succeed – because free time is the scarcest commodity upon this planet these days. No one has much free time, and whatever free time we do have, gets gobbled by all the various life pressures loudly demanding our attention. The only way to set aside half an hour for the daily attraction meditation is to solidly write this event into your daily calendar – and regularly reinforce your intent to make the fulfilment of your love life vital to each new day's activities. Of course, some days you'll encounter difficulties and complications that will eat into your precious half hour – but in general, you will need to be very firm in insisting that no one and no outside pressure impinge on your half-hour meditation routine.

I recommend that you go right now and get pen and paper, and write the time schedule for everything you do. And on this time schedule, see if you can find half an hour – or at the minimum fifteen minutes – to pause and move through the attraction meditation. If at all possible, please do this right now, and begin actively to create time for your heart's deepest needs.

pause . . . breathe . . . reflect . . . experience

Your Daily Attraction Meditation

Most people find it best, when setting up a daily meditation routine, to retreat to the same quiet place each day, so that the place you meditate helps reinforce the ongoing growth and new experience you're opening up to. So if at all possible, see if you can return to the same place for your meditation, day in and day out. Of course sometimes you'll have to do your meditation elsewhere, but set a general goal of returning to a quiet comfortable location of your choosing, when you pause for your attraction meditation.

I'm going to present you now with the formal structure of the attraction meditation, drawn from what you've already learned in earlier chapters. Naturally, you're free to modify any part of this meditation if the words don't quite reflect your life philosophy, or some other bother makes you want to ad lib with the words I'm offering. You can also choose your own pace to move through the meditation – I'm just giving general guidelines that work for most.

At first, you'll probably need to have the book open to guide you through this full process, or be listening to me guiding you through the process. Hold in mind that you're now in the learning phase of this programme – it does take a bit of time to learn by heart a process such as this one. For now you'll want to read a short passage, then pause and turn inward to experience it. Then when you're ready you can open your eyes and read the next short passage or focus phrase, and turn inward again for at least a few breaths . . . you'll find that you can move quite deeply into insight and power, even when you're still in the phase of referring to the book for your next step . . .

FULL ATTRACTION MEDITATION

Find a quiet time and place where you can enjoy the bliss and empowerment of entering the deep state of harmony found in this meditation. Set aside fifteen to forty-five minutes when you have plenty of time to relax . . . Remember that nurturing the feeling of effortless joy is the key inner quality to encourage here ... no pushing, just enjoyable exploration, with a new experience coming to you each time:

◆ Make sure you're feeling comfortable in your body to start out with – feel free to stretch all you want, and yawn ... let your body move as it wants to, to discharge tensions.

◆ Tune into the air flowing in and out your nose (or mouth) as you breathe ... expand your awareness to include the movements in your chest and belly as your breaths come and go and come again ... and gently expand your awareness to include the feelings in your heart, right in the middle of your breathing.

◆ Accept whatever feelings you find right now, breathe into them, let them change with each new breath ...

◆ Expand your awareness to include your whole body, here in this present moment. Be aware of your toes ... your hands ... your throat ... your pelvis ... your knees ... your belly ... allow your awareness to move around your body and find places that feel especially good right now ... enjoy the good feelings you find ... move all you want to let these good feelings expand ...

◆ Bring your focus to your breathing again ... open more to the feelings in your heart ... and begin to think of someone in your life whom you love. Let your love for this person fill your heart as you aim your attention towards this person, wherever they may be – they will feel your attention when you aim it towards them ... they can feel your love ... enjoy this heart-to-heart communion ...

◆ And now you can shift into receive mode in your heart, so that you begin to feel the love this person has for you ... open your heart, and let their love come in ...

◆ And open your heart more as you let all the pure spiritual love of the universe come flowing into your heart ... with every new breath, be open to receive more love, until your whole heart and being fills with love ... relax and enjoy this vibrant loving feeling ...

◆ And now, gently return your attention to your breaths, coming and going . . . and begin to say the following focus phrases that will awaken new experiences in your heart, mind and soul . . .

1. Yearning

The feelings in your heart are the power you have to heal . . . to reach out . . . to manifest your lover . . . after saying each of these focus phrases, pause and see how you feel in your heart, about the intent you just stated:

'I want to heal my emotional wounds . . .'
'I feel a deep yearning for new love . . .'
'I am going to attract new love to me . . .'

~ pause & experience ~

2. Forgiving and Healing

It's time to let go . . . to accept . . . to forgive . . . and to open up and receive healing and love . . . say the intent . . . experience the reverberations of the words . . .

'I accept and love myself, just as I am.'
'I forgive and let go of my old lovers.'
'My heart is open to receive . . . healing . . . and love.'

~ pause & experience ~

3. Waking Up Sexually

You are as beautiful as you feel inside . . . let yourself feel good . . . let the world see you as attractive and powerful and full of love . . .

'I am a beautiful powerful sexual being.'
'I give myself permission to feel good in my body.'
'See me – sexually attractive . . . ready for love.'

~ pause & experience ~

4. Charging

Now let's focus specifically on the passion you feel inside your body, in your heart, in your belly, in your genitals, in your throat – in your whole body. Say the statements one by one, breathe . . . and pause to experience whatever new feelings and insights come to you . . .

'I feel passion . . . in my heart . . . in my belly. . .'
'I feel sexual hunger in my genitals . . . in my throat. . .'
'My whole being is charged with loving energy.'

~ pause & experience ~

5. Broadcasting

It's time to let the world know you're here and you're ready for your true love. Say it – do it! Let these words empower you . . . wake up the world to your desire . . . and aim your intent directly towards that person out there who is also aiming towards you . . .

'Here I am right now, yearning for love.'
'I am reaching out to you . . .'
'Feel me . . . come into my life.'

~ pause & experience ~

6. Surrendering

Now let's move deeper . . . allow your thoughts to become quiet . . . your breathing even and deep . . . and go ahead and ask for help and guidance . . . open your entire being to the greater loving force that will bring your heart together with your lover-to-be . . .

'My mind is quiet . . . my breathing calm.'
'I request help from my deeper source.'
'I surrender to spiritual wisdom and guidance.'

~ pause & experience ~

7. Moving Towards Encounter

And now go all the way . . . open up to experience connection with
your lover . . . say it . . . experience it . . . from the depths of your
heart, say the following statements . . . pause after each one . . .
breathe . . . experience . . .

'I let go of inhibitions . . .'
'I need you . . . I love you . . .'
'Here I am – I feel you!'

~ pause & experience ~

◆ And now you can just relax . . . stay with your feelings . . . allow
your breaths to deepen . . . and as you hold your heart open to your
new lover, feel in your whole body what this person is like . . . as if
you are already in your lover's arms . . . look deeply into your lover's
eyes . . . see your lover's soul . . . and feel how you are together
already in spirit . . .

◆ You can stay in meditation for as long as you want . . . and when
you're ready you can open your eyes . . . stretch and yawn . . . and
as you go about your day, be spontaneous in where you go . . . so
that your two bodies can move closer and closer towards each other
. . . let spirit move you through your day . . . as you come closer to
suddenly encountering each other . . . looking into each other's eyes
. . . and knowing – that you have found your true love!

pause . . . breathe . . . reflect . . . experience

Chapter 9

Hunt Of The Heart

Here's how I see your present scenario – you are now in the process of establishing a daily attraction-meditation routine that will move you through the seven steps of daily preparation needed for optimum power to connect with and attract your lover and heart and deeper energetic and spiritual dimensions. With such a core daily practice becoming well established and in progress, it's time to talk about what you're going to be doing, when you're not quietly in retreat in the attraction meditation.

In using the word 'hunt' we're of course not talking about going out and hunting anything with a gun or striving nobly to bring meat home for the family. We're talking about the hunt of the heart – where each and every moment when you're out and around in the world fulfilling your daily routine, you're also consciously moving yourself into position for a significant encounter – if you're in the right state of mind.

I grew up on a cattle ranch where my father and my grandfather and my great-grandfather before me had seriously mastered the traditional deer-hunt methodology and mindset, mixing ancient Chumash Indian approaches to hunting with the more modern European approach. And although my generation came to mostly reject deer hunting as a once vital but now unnecessary act of violence in our food-gathering process (which means we now let the slaughterhouse do our killing), I did learn quite deeply the underlying mind management necessary for succeeding in the proverbial hunt. I have found the ancient stalking tradition essentially congruent with what we're talking about in this context – the romantic hunt of the heart.

Here's what seems most important for you to reflect upon, and perhaps integrate into your own approach to actually going out and hunting for true love, within the context of the psychological and spiritual dimensions of finding true love that we've been discussing. First of all, before a hunter leaves the house to physically begin the hunt, much mental preparation is required. You need to be very clear in your intent – yes, you are going out with the clear purpose of finding, and taking home with you, the target of your hunt. In your case you've already explored (at least as a beginning) your intent to make contact with and come together with a special person 'out there' who will satisfy your hungers – in this case, for sexual and romantic fulfilment.

The second thing a hunter does before heading off into the heat of the hunt, is to make sure that his or her emotions are clear and positive, so that there will be no disruption of the hunt based on feelings of confusion, uncertainty, anger, depression or apprehension. You are also in the process each and every new day, of focusing on your unfinished and unhealed emotional turmoil from the past, so that you can let go of negative thoughts and emotions and focus entirely on the present moment where you'll find your heart's desire in the flesh.

The third step a hunter must make before going into physical action, is that of making contact, in his or her heart, with the living being that is out there, destined for an encounter with the hunter. In traditional American Indian deer hunting, the hunter quite openly establishes heart contact with the deer – and knows that the deer is hunting him just as much as he is hunting the deer. Included strongly in this sense of contact with the deer is a vital respect for the life that is going to be taken, and thankfulness that Great Spirit is providing the hunter with food and materials to feed and clothe his family. In native times, there was indeed no separation between physical and spiritual – it was all one greater reality that the Indian participated humbly within. And in similar spirit, you're learning in your daily meditations to merge heart, mind and spirit into one greater consciousness that will guide you towards your hunt's conclusion.

When these three primary mental and emotional preparations have been fulfilled, then and only then does the hunter feel ready to take the fourth step – and enter into movement in the outside world. Now the hunt formally begins, and from the first steps the hunter takes, there is the clear sense that for every step the hunter takes, the hunted is also taking a step – and these steps of hunter and hunted are moving inextricably towards each other and the encounter that will climax the hunt.

In like spirit, except for when you're sitting quietly moving through your seven-step attraction meditation, you are in movement in the world, taking step after step throughout your day, all the while maintaining your hunter's mental and emotional awareness, calm and yet alert, relaxed and yet at any moment ready to respond when you suddenly perceive what you're hunting for.

By definition, you don't know the time or the place where your true love is going to suddenly appear. Nor does your true love know. You're both caught up in a great mystery adventure as you stalk each other, perhaps passing each other ten or fifty times as each day you get on the same subway or walk the hallways of the same building. Often in the traditional hunt, the Indian and the deer would pass quite close by but not notice each other – but all the while the readiness is present and the hunt ongoing.

How do you feel about being a hunter – or about having someone hunting for you? The reality is this – if you're not able to consciously take on the role of romantic hunter, and actually thrive in the mystery and excitement (and yes, sometimes the tedium and struggles) of the hunt, you're not going to have much success in finding what you're hunting for. Many women especially don't want to see themselves as hunters, nor do they want to feel like they're the hunted. All sorts of negative childhood attitudes and media distortions of the nature of being the hunter and the hunted have polluted their deeper roles.

So please, take some time to reconsider your initial reaction to seeing yourself as a hunter of the heart. Be honest about your romantic goals, and what you want to accomplish – and then adopt the role that will enable you to accomplish your goal. Pause a few moments now, and reflect upon how you feel about being a hunter . . .

pause . . . breathe . . . reflect . . . experience

Shopping versus Hunting

Probably every day, you put on your hunter mental gear and head out on the hunt – for something or other. Even if you're just needing some crackers and cheese and a bottle of wine, as soon as you hold the particular desire and intent in your mind, and choose to go out into the world to find what you need, you've become the hunter.

I challenge you to begin to be conscious of your usual hunting habits, for whatever you're seeking out there. Notice your mind's usual habits when you become aware of something you need. Observe your behaviour, the next few days, as you hunt one thing after another. Do you enjoy the hunt? Are you good at it? What are the steps you move through, from the time you have a need or desire, to the time you find the solution to that need or desire? Don't judge yourself as a good or bad hunter – just observe your habits of mind and movement, the thoughts and emotions that arise when you recognize an unfulfilled need, and your behaviour as you go about fulfilling that need.

Often I hear women talking about 'shopping for a man'. Yes, there are great parallels between shopping and hunting. So every time you go out shopping, watch how you go about it. And ask yourself the following questions, to stimulate insights into how you shop/hunt, and whether you might want to change any of your habitual ways of shopping, as you go hunting for your lover:

ONE: Do you find shopping fun, or are you an impatient shopper?

TWO: Do you put off shopping for something, or immediately go into action?

THREE: Are you a lucky shopper, or is it hard work to find what you want?

FOUR: Do you settle for second best, or keep looking for exactly what you want?

FIVE: Is heading off on a shopping trip fun, or a bother?

SIX: How do you usually feel when you find what you were looking for?

SEVEN: When you get home, are you usually pleased with what you found?

Many people have negative attitudes about shopping, and these negative attitudes can directly infiltrate and interfere with their search for romantic fulfilment. If you find that shopping carries negative connotations, or that you have shopping habits that make the very process no fun at all, you're going to want to separate your shopping habits from your hunting-for-love habits. Moving through the attraction meditation each day will be of great help in turning your attention regularly towards positive hunting attitudes. Observing your usual shopping habits will also provoke insight, and change. The power of your loving attention towards your habits is the primary force that perceives where change is needed, and then generates the insights into how to change your behaviour to your advantage.

In shopping, you are clearly the action person, and the object you're wanting to buy is the passive presence in the game. This is where the hunt of the heart is quite different from shopping – because the person you're hunting is also hunting for you, which makes the game so much more exciting. Plus, you can't just get out your credit card when you find your new true love – you've got to get out your heart instead, and pay for true love with your attention, your presence, your whole being.

The magic of true love is that the exchange that happens for you to get each other is equal to and empowered by a force vastly greater than money – love itself.

Action Time Is Here

I don't want to push you over-early out into the hunt of the heart. You know by now how deeply I value the preparatory action that you make first, in dedicating yourself to the first section of this book and the attraction-meditation process. If you want to spend a few weeks focusing entirely on the preparation phase before even considering the hunt itself, that's perfectly fine and normal. But let's at least talk through the second phase, when you combine daily meditation time with action-hunting time. And for those of you who're ready right now to get out and actively stalk your lover as your lover stalks you, here's my advice on how to best approach this exciting experience:

HuntNote 1: Don't feel in a hurry. You cannot push the hunt by being impatient or overly expectant. Yes, you're going to feel excited and eager – but you also have to accept that your hunt could take two hours or two years. Therefore, what's vital is enjoying each moment of the hunt!

HuntNote 2: Successful hunters are devotees of breath awareness. You will find your new lover only in the intensity of the eternal present moment. You don't want to drift off into thoughts of the past or the future – when you're on the hunt, it's vital to be here and now, where the discovery experience will happen. And staying aware of your breathing is the best way to stay in the here and now. This means that you want to take with you on the hunt the basic breath-awareness process you're mastering in your attraction meditation.

HuntNote 3: Recognizing your true love when you see him or her is a seemingly magical discovery process that, as we've seen, requires an integration of your senses and your heart. Neurological evidence now shows that when you receive a visual image, that visual information goes not only to your brain, but also to your heart. You do see with your heart as well as your head – and only if you're actively aware of your heart are you going to recognize the heart you're seeking . . . through looking into that person's eyes. So you want to hunt not only with your eyes, but with your heart as well.

HuntNote 4: Remember that there is someone out there hunting for you now too – and your appearance, your sexual presence, and your deeper heart emanations are very important to help this person recognize you. So equally with your outward focus of the hunter, you need to also maintain an inner focus of your own presence and attractive power. Fifty per cent of your hunting time should be devoted not to active seeking, but to passive (yet powerful) pauses in which you return to your own love for yourself, and your inner feelings of powerful yearning and readiness.

HuntNote 5: Successful hunting requires that you break regularly from your normal habits of movement and perception, so that you throw yourself into new territory, and perceive the world around you in new ways. If you just run in your usual routines, your chance of encountering someone in their routines is quite low. You have to set yourself free to respond spontaneously to impulse. You need to become an explorer of the world again, open to new experience. Only with a flair of adventure will you find the new adventure of your life.

In a slightly different format, here are the five HuntNotes for you to pause now and reflect upon. Remember to first tune into your breathing . . . the feelings in your heart . . . your whole body here in this present moment. And in this expanded state, read each of the following statements, and see what insights and feelings are provoked by saying the sentences:

HuntNote 1: 'I shall be relaxed and patient in my hunt for true love.'

HuntNote 2: 'I will stay aware of my breathing while out on the hunt.'

HuntNote 3: 'I will hold my heart as central, as I look for my new life partner.'

HuntNote 4: 'I will keep myself feeling attractive and passionate for love.'

HuntNote 5: 'I will venture into spontaneous new adventures during my hunt.'

pause . . . breathe . . . reflect . . . experience

Meditation In Action

I've spent a lot of my professional life exploring the fascinating fact that meditation isn't just something we do half an hour a day off in a closet totally cut off from our everyday life. Yes, it's good to develop that half-hour practice, as we've explored earlier, and I hope that you do – because on all fronts, people's lives tend to improve dramatically when they add a bit of conscious mind management of the spiritual variety to their daily routines. The quiet observance of our thoughts, the meditative quieting of our minds, and the purposeful refocusing of our attention in valuable directions all lead to greater peace, insight, health, and success in life.

At the same time, to put aside everything you've learned in quiet meditation, and go out into the world with your same old mental habits and emotional chaos, seems highly unproductive – compared to the bright possibility of bringing your meditation with you as you re-enter the fray of daily life. Who says you can't remain acutely aware of your breathing while you're at work, or on a date, or commuting? Why can't you stay deeply attuned to the feelings in your heart when you're talking with a friend, mowing the lawn, or washing the dishes? And what's to keep you from staying in whole-body consciousness in the present moment, in touch with all your deeper spiritual powers, while sitting in a meeting or shopping for groceries? And to the point – why not bring all the pluses you're gaining, mind-management-wise, with you when you head off into the wild woolly world seeking your beloved?

What I'm suggesting is quite simple. While in your daily half-hour retreat, practise the mind-management techniques taught in this book. And as you get up and go on about your day, take these techniques with you. Meditating simply means being conscious, in the present moment, of what's happening. Mind management means choosing where you're going to direct your attention, moment to moment. And nowhere do you need these two qualities more than when you're out searching for your loved one.

I'm not saying that right away, you can remain in a highly conscious state every moment of the day. Of course you're going to get sucked off into memories, fantasies, worries and problem-solving quite often – and there's nothing wrong with these other activities of the mind, as long as you regularly return your attention to the experience of the present moment, and plug back into the emerging reality where your lover will suddenly at some point – appear!

The issue is this – just how strong is your desire to find your true love? If you don't really care if you find this special person tomorrow or next year, then it doesn't really matter that much if you go through most of your day mostly unconscious of your breathing, your heart, and your interaction with new people around you. Only your own intensity of romantic yearning will determine how seriously you take what I'm saying here. The challenge is up to you – to continue drifting through your day with your old mental habits sucking you off into the past and the future most of the time; or to actively take control of your own mind, and choose to hold your awareness in the here and now where new experience (and new lovers) are to be found.

Even as you're reading these words, as I keep pointing out, you can be aware of your breathing, your heart, your whole body here in this present moment. You never lose anything by holding your mind in expanded mode – you always gain. Laziness, fear and conditioning hold you in relative contraction awareness-wise. Desire, courage and the will to advance and change your life for the better, push you into the new. And every new moment, you have the choice.

Right now – with this new breath of air flowing in your nose, and this new movement in your chest and belly as you exhale, and this new feeling in your heart – you can maximize your hunting potential so that your presence radiates outward towards your lover, and your senses successfully scan the outside world . . . to receive and respond to your lover's presence.

See how it feels in your heart and whole body, to say the following:

'I choose to manage my mind so that I expand my everyday awareness.'

'I choose to live more in the present moment, so I can find my lover faster.'

'I choose to feel vibrant and radiate my presence – to help my lover find me.'

'I choose to be more spontaneous, every moment of each new day.'

'I choose with each new breath, to be actively hunting for my new partner.'

pause . . . breathe . . . reflect . . . experience

Eyes Of The Hunter

You don't know what your new lover will look like. Whatever visual image of his or her lips, eyes, mouth, hair or body-build you might be holding is a visual image that will get in your way of recognizing the person you're looking for. This is a very curious dilemma in romance – you're hunting for someone but you don't have any idea what they look like. If you had a photo of them, then you'd surely want to scan the faces of everyone you meet, trying to match features and thus make a positive identification. And you'd manage your visual activity in such a way as to maximize your image-processing speed and accuracy.

We're well trained in this sort of visual activity – the search-and-find function of seeing where we're rapidly comparing present visual inputs with our memory-bank images, looking for a positive match. We're much less trained in the fine art of looking with our hearts – looking to see the whole person and to sense that person's radiating energy field. This is not how we find that box of noodles or that can of soda. But it is how we find the love of our life.

And this is one of the main reasons I've called this book 'Let Love Find You', because in essence, as I've mentioned before, what you're looking for is love. You're trying to sense a similar energy field to yours, out there in the world somewhere. You're meeting people's eyes not to associate those eyes with past eyes you've seen, but rather to look so deeply into those eyes that you can see the heart and soul of the person. And this type of looking requires, as we've been exploring, that your own eyes be deeply attuned with your own heart and soul. What we have here are two hearts looking out through two pairs of eyes, sensing ineffable but very real heart qualities that resonate so strongly together, we know instantly – it's a match!

You will want to begin seeing the world with eyes that carry this depth. In general, this is the best way to go about life. If we all let everyone look to our souls and feel our loving presence, what a wonderful world it would be. And I encourage you, as you move about the face of the earth each new day, to look into all eyes to perceive kindred souls out there. Don't just be looking for your ideal mate. Be open to respond to whoever out there is similar enough to you to awaken your heart with the instant response of a slight smile of recognition.

The thing about finding true love is this – sometimes yes, you suddenly turn a corner and there your lover is. But more often than not, you will meet your true love through an intermediary who brings you together – and you want to respond to that intermediary as well as to the final resolution of your search. I would never have met my wife, for instance, if I hadn't first met a publisher with wonderful deep eyes and heart, who introduced me to an equally wonderful fellow who arranges seminars in Switzerland, who introduced me to the wonderful couple who loaned me their house for a week – upon whose door my true love rapped her lovely knuckles that fated evening.

In this mysterious way, love finds us. Through being observant, open and responsive to the presence of like-minded folk whoever they may be, we participate in the dance of the heart, and come closer to our fated encounter. So as you go out into the world later today, or tomorrow, and each new day, I do challenge you to leap into a new relationship with the outside world. Lead with your heart. Let people see into your soul. Trust the universe to have a greater game plan for your movements each new moment. Let your feet walk where they will, and respond to the whims and inclinations of your fancy so that spirit can move you. And when you see love, respond with love – let your light shine, and surely, love shall find you!

To end this chapter, close your eyes after reading this paragraph, and imagine that you're headed out into the world tomorrow morning. Imagine what you're going to do inside your own mind and heart, so that you're a hunter who's also open to being hunted . . . imagine looking in people's eyes, and seeing with your heart . . . and letting people see into your soul through your eyes . . . and whole-body presence . . .

pause . . . breathe . . . reflect . . . experience

Chapter 10

Unattached To Outcomes

Successful hunters are the ones who know how to remain content inside their own skins, and take whatever happens each new day with equanimity. In the hunt of the heart, you're naturally going to encounter any number of people who temporarily seem to make sparks fly romantically – only to fizzle quickly into nothing. You can't tell until you explore a bit, if the romantic spark is going to turn into a forest fire of passion, or disappear through mutual disinterest or other reason. With this in mind it's vital, right in the heat of the hunt, to know how to remain relatively unattached to outcomes.

I've been gently teaching you how to master an inner state of quiescence that comes from being your own friend first, and accepting the present moment fully, just as it is. Over and over, successful couples talk about how both of then had already attained the heart quality where they were no longer needy, before they met their true love. Because they felt whole inside their own hearts already, they weren't nervously grabbing at the first chance for romance that came to them. Therefore they were able to relax and allow the present moment to unfold however it would, rather than trying to push and 'make a relationship happen' with someone who wasn't highly matched to their needs and temperament. They could be patient, and allow love to find them without undue stress and confusion.

In this chapter let's explore in further depth how to remain cool and calm right in the midst of the romantic hunt. From the very first chapter you've been learning how to love yourself and be content with the present moment, rather than overly fixated on pushing towards the future. Successful hunting often requires letting go entirely of any future dream, in order to participate in an unexpected present moment with many twists and turns that lead to an entirely new situation and encounter opportunity.

I remember when Birgitta and I first came together in Solothurn and experienced our giant flash of recognition. Yes, we were both keenly aware that something momentous had happened in our lives – but at the same time, neither of us was needy enough emotionally to want to plunge into an instant overwhelming love affair. We'd both been through whirlwind involvements that had left us crashed and lonely and in extreme emotional pain because of jumping in too fast too deep. So instead, we spent a full six months holding our distance in some ways, and consciously staying open to the possibility that we might part. Thus, by remaining unattached to the outcome of our relationship we were able to fully explore each other in the present moment, and not fool ourselves in the name of love.

What is your romantic track record in this regard? In the past, when you've fallen in love have you plunged fast and furious, craving to lose yourself in the other person – or have you already mastered the fine art of loving yourself first, and holding your heart's centre in your own chest rather than giving it to a lover?

Pause and close your eyes after reading this paragraph, and see what memories and insights come – what has been your past experience . . . and what do you want for your coming experience?

pause . . . breathe . . . reflect . . . experience

Gently Shattering The 'Oneness' Myth

I'm going to say something now that might make you very upset with me but I need to say it anyway, so it's out on the table for open examination. There does exist a vast difference between puppy love, and mature love. Yes, as teenagers we all get hit hard in our first sexual relationships because we do tend to totally surrender our separate sense of self and lose ourselves in the other person. We give up our independent centre altogether and regress back to a quality of oneness we shared with our mother. Certainly in the womb we were mostly one with our mother, and this was our first experience of love. As we grew up we grew away from that love with our mother – but some part of us still hungered to get back to that wombian feeling of boundary-less love. And in our first wild love affairs as teenagers we tended to plunge into that wombian feeling.

Those early teen love affairs, even though in some ways the most intense of a lifetime, almost never end up as long-lasting relationships – because mature relating is so very different from puppy love where our love object becomes absolutely everything, and is seen as a perfect embodiment of romantic fulfilment. We tended to project an idealized image onto our all-too-mortal lover, and in so doing, doomed the relationship to playing out its intense fantasy of perfect love, until the illusory bubble popped and the affair suddenly came to a calamitous end.

My experience is that human beings learn quite slowly, when it comes to love. I myself certainly kept repeating the puppy-love approach to relationships, well into my late twenties until finally my heart got broken so terribly that I had to say – never again. No more lovers, please, that make me feel like I can't live without them. No more relationships where I feel that I'll die if I'm deserted by my true love. No more regressions back to wombian feelings, even if those feelings are so ultimately wonderful. Enough is enough – no more agony of the heart!

I don't know where you are, on this progression from being an infant totally dependent on your mother's love and acceptance, to where you have found your own inner centre that's grounded not on another person's love and acceptance, but on your own love and acceptance that you give to yourself. Wherever you are on this progression, I encourage you to reflect upon what you really want in your next relationship. Are you still seeking someone to take the place of your mother or father, someone to make everything okay and give you the feeling of being loved that you can't yet give yourself? Or are you ready to say, enough idealized love – enough pain and suffering caused by giving your own centre of being to another person to take care of forever . . .

For me, true love means loving someone for who they are and what they need in life, not for what you need and what they're giving you. This means that if you really love someone, and their path begins to lead away from you, you have held your own centre so that you can still love them, if they say it's time to go away from you. That's what it means to really love someone – and that's the love of a mature relationship where each person continues to nurture their own independent self, so that a freedom remains where love isn't dependence, where compassion isn't dulled by the fear of losing one's love object.

We'll be exploring this general issue of love and freedom in the coming chapters because it's so very important to successful relating. For now, let's hold our focus tightly on the initial issue that you're exploring, about becoming your own best friend so that even when you're alone, you can feel okay in your heart, and feel whole in your soul.

If you have consciously strengthened this emotional and spiritual muscle before you meet your true love, you'll be in strong position to maintain your independent centre when the lightning strikes. Plus, if you're already your own best friend, you'll tend to attract a lover who is also his or her own best friend – and voila! A mature and very hopeful relationship will have the chance to begin to form, centred around two independent people who are in love and yet, at the same time, able to live on their own – that's freedom!

Do you agree with what I'm saying about preserving your own separate heart centre even in the heat of new love? Or do you feel that romantic love must always involve the loss of your individual separate centre, and the formation of a relationship based on total oneness and that wonderful wombian feeling you had and then lost, as an infant? Pause, look to your breathing, and expand to be aware of whatever feelings you find in your heart right now . . . and see what insights come to you!

Pause . . . breathe . . . reflect . . . experience

Maximize Your Options

Life in general, and especially our tumultuous love life, all too often seems riddled with paradox when we first start to consciously explore what makes things happen in life, and what we can do to influence the outcome of situations we're in to our advantage. I've told you how important it is to clarify your desires and intent, so that you know clearly what it is you want in life. Without applying your willpower to get what you want, usually you just don't get it – period. But at the same time, you hear me now saying that even while you're actively hunting to find what you need in life, you must remain calm and un-attached to what happens. What's going on here?

In oriental philosophies, paradox is considered the higher-order reality of life. I remember one of my Zen teachers, Alan Watts, teaching me what he considered his major breakthrough – that the only way to make sense of life at deeper levels where paradox seems to rule, is to expand your concept of reality from one hundred per cent to two hundred per cent. Yes, it's a hundred per cent true that you must use willpower and intent, and actively go hunting for what you need in life. But it's also a hundred per cent true that for that hunt to be truly successful, you must remain unattached to the outcome of your hunt. Both truths co-exist, in the greater reality of life.

You've seen how important intent is, as you harness your desires and yearnings and point your attention and energy directly towards attaining the goal you have set. You want to find a deep love, and you are in training to actively go out and find what you're seeking. But at the same time, I'm now saying, even in the heat of the hunt, and also when you think you might have found true love, it's important not to get consumed in completing your mission and attached to the idea that things must work out the way you want them to.

Here's how it works. Yes, you prepare yourself and attract the desired love in your direction. And yes, you go out and actively hunt what and who you're seeking. And at the same time, you make sure you don't let the concept in your head determine what happens. When you are attached to the outcome of a situation, you're really attached to your idea of what you think should happen – and that idea in your head is never going to quite match the reality that's emerging. Your ideas and imaginations of what you want to happen in your life in the future are after all based only on past events that you then project into a vision of what might happen in the future. So as long as you're attached to attaining your vision in your mind of what you think should happen, you're actually stuck in the past and in your head – you're not participating in the unfolding of a unique new moment and relationship.

Being unattached to the outcome of a situation means letting go of your mind's fantasies of what might satisfy you, so that you can embrace the unique new happening that's coming to you in the present moment. You can't know what the outcome of a situation should be, until it happens. And as long as you're attached to life unfolding according to an ideal game plan you're holding in your mind, you're not free to participate in the unique new experience happening as the new moment unfolds.

It's always nice if life unfolds almost exactly as we envision it unfolding – but usually it doesn't. And here's the rub. If you only open your heart to events that unfold in accordance to your inner dream of how things should happen, you're going to remain limited to your vision, and miss out on all the great happenings that are different from your mental projections, but capable of deeply satisfying you nonetheless. You limit yourself when you're attached to a particular outcome in a new situation. You set yourself free to maximize your options when you're unattached to outcomes and open to embrace quite new events – that you never could have imagined (because they've never happened to you before) but that perfectly soothe and satisfy your heart's yearnings.

Lonely people tend to sit around dreaming and fantasizing about their ideal lover, and the ideal romantic encounter that initiates a new relationship. Surely such fantasizing is healthy and fine to indulge in sometimes. But please be aware of the fact that when your mind is full of ideal fantasies about how you want your life to unfold, you're actively shutting yourself off from a myriad of unique events that might come to you, that don't fit your fantasy but perhaps transcend your imagination tenfold. We tend to see and get what we expect and accept – so the trick is to let go of being attached to limiting expectations, and stay open to the new.

Letting Love Happen

Specifically in the world of romantic love, our tendency as we hunt our true love and stay open to letting love find us, is to create in our minds a fairly fixed idea of what it is we want to have happen, and the sort of person we want to have it happen with. This is entirely natural, and in moderation perfectly fine. You need a general sense of what it is you're looking for and what you want to have happen, in order to aim your attention in that general area of manifestation.

And at the same time, you can also manage your mind so that you spend minimum time dreaming and fantasizing (which are products of your memory and past events projected into a fantasy vision of the future), and maximum time in the present moment focused on the actual experience coming to you in the here and now. As I've been teaching over and over, you can choose to tune into your senses, which hold you in experiential mode, rather than drifting into cognitive processes that shift you into the past and future.

In other words, you can embrace what God brings you each new moment, rather than trying to fulfil your limited ego drives. Said another way, you can trust the greater guidance in your life to know what will truly satisfy you, rather than being driven by your ego's concept of what you need.

I mentioned earlier that right at the moment when I met my true love, my mind was momentarily stuck between ignoring this woman as a future love because she didn't look at all like I had envisioned my true love to look like, or putting aside the outcome I had envisioned in my life, and opening up to explore whether this unique creature before me just might be even more wonderful than what I'd imagined. By choosing to be unattached to the imagined outcome I'd anticipated in my life, I was able to enter into a qualitatively new relationship that vastly transcended my mind's expectation.

Likewise after Birgitta and I first met, I watched part of my mind holding tight to my imagined outcome of a particular type of relationship. Birgitta didn't fit the pattern I expected and thought I wanted based on past relationships. So what was I to do, let go of my expectations, or let go of this woman?

The choice, when you see it clearly, is quite definite. Are you going to refuse any relationship that doesn't match what you're expecting – or are you going to let go of your imagined outcome, and plunge into something beautifully new?

Take a few moments now, to pause and reflect on this vital question of becoming unattached to outcomes in romantic love. Are you ready to allow events to happen and trust life to bring you a unique new love, or are you determined to accept into your life only those people and events that fit your predetermined image of true love?

pause . . . breathe . . . reflect . . . experience

Openness To The Unexpected

Most of us who are yearning for true love have already endured a number of casual affairs that ended quite soon, and left an empty feeling inside. Most of us have also become caught up in a wild flurry of passion in a love affair that seemed destined to last forever – only to suddenly have the affair explode and come to an untimely death with all the agony of a seriously broken heart. And so, naturally, most of us seeking a new relationship are hoping that this relationship will be the one that lasts forever, so we never have to go through a broken heart again.

It's most wonderful to discover and nurture and enjoy a lasting love relationship. Much of this book is preparing you for just such an enduring sexual partnership. However, I feel the great need right now to also praise the short-term or mid-term relationship, if it's entered into properly and ended properly so that the proverbial devastating heartbreak doesn't have to mar the experience.

When I look back I can remember four special deep relationships that didn't last all that long, but that wonderfully touched my heart, expanded my sense of who I am, and brought a quality of love into my life that was unique – and that continues to resonate in my heart eternally. We never know when we enter into a relationship, how long it will last. The fated duration of the merger of two souls in sexual love is determined by forces beyond our limited perception of life. And only if we enter into the relationship unattached to outcomes, can we readily accept when relationships end sooner than we anticipated.

Who knows what gift a person has to give us? Who knows what special gift of healing, insight, awakening and wisdom we have to give to another person, just through being who we are with them? And who can say how long it takes for these gifts to be given, before we move on again in our separate directions?

When we enter into a relationship determined to attach ourselves to the other person permanently, we set ourselves up for the possibility of serious heartbreak. When we enter into a relationship, regardless of the passion, determined to stay unattached to the outcome of the relationship, we minimize our possibility of serious heartbreak, and maximize our opportunity to give and receive deep gifts of the heart. As I mentioned before, true love is not possessive. True love sets the other person free to come and go as their inner guide directs them.

You also have the right to expect from a new lover, this sense of your also being free to live your life guided by a deeper directive than committing to a mutually possessive co-dependent relationship (that ends up shy on love and loaded with negative emotions such as fear, possessiveness, guilt and so forth). Even before you meet your next lover, you will serve yourself and that new lover best by getting clear in your heart that freedom in a relationship is golden.

When both of you are unattached to the outcome of the relationship, you're free to allow that relationship to naturally develop and evolve, and determine its own duration. You set the higher forces of the universe free to act in your lives and guide you into vastly more expansive and fulfilling feelings and experiences than you would receive if you remain attached to a particular outcome and deny all other outcomes of the relationship.

See how you feel in your heart, when you say the following sentences. Tune into your breathing . . . your heart . . . your whole body here in the present moment, and after you say each sentence, allow the words to awaken insights and feelings that shed light on how you feel about freedom in relating. See if you agree or disagree with the statement, and reflect upon your own present attitudes and expectations:

'I won't share my heart unless I'm sure the relationship's going to last forever.'

'Even a short deep love affair can bring wonderful positive experiences.'

'I'm terribly afraid to risk having my heart broken again.'

'I'm not attached to the outcome of new love encounters.'

'I trust the wisdom of the Universe to determine who I should be with next.'

'I won't accept anything but a total permanent sexual partnership.'

'I can stay free in my heart, even while loving someone deeply.'

And now, after exploring how you feel about freedom in love, you can just relax . . . tune into your breaths coming and going . . . let your breathing stop when it wants to . . . and start when it wants to . . . set your breathing free . . . and tune into your heart, and set your heart free . . . as you say to yourself, *'I trust my higher guide to bring me whatever love I'm ready for . . . I am unattached to outcomes . . . I surrender to love.'*

pause . . . breathe . . . reflect . . . experience

Chapter 11

Managing The Excitement

There's no separating sexual arousal from romantic love - and there's equally no way to take the wild rush of excitement out of the hunt for a sexual mate. Actively pushing for sexual encounter and fulfilment happens to be just about the most exciting thing we can imagine doing, except perhaps for leaping from a plane at ten thousand feet for the first time ...

Whatever else we might be, we are all of us sexual to the core of our being, packing an inescapable, genetically programmed, regularly renewable charge of energy in our bodies – that crazy lustful passion of our primal sex drive. Yes, we might be spiritual creatures who can leap up and make direct mystic heart contact with our Creator – but at the same time, that same Creator has programmed us with an innate sexual desire and compulsion to seek out a sexual mate, and then plunge into the steaming abyss of erotic abandon and total orgasmic discharge with that mate.

Why is it so inherently exciting to approach the sexual act? For me this answer is equally biochemical and spiritual. Our biological animal instinct to seek out and have sex comes programmed with a host of quite radical hormonal shifts that transform our experience in our bodies, and thus our emotions and minds as well. I won't bother you with the academic details but I'm sure you've already felt what I'm talking about from the inside out. The act of approaching and entering into a sexual union provokes an acceleration of the heartbeat, a tensing and then a deepening of the breathing, a flush of blood to the face and genitals, a hunger in the mouth and throat, a wild growing desire in the groin, and a decidedly compulsive fixation on nothing except the attainment of more and more sexual stimulation until the whole body is crazy with pleasure and desire and the push for release and orgasm.

Wow.

And this is what you're asking for.

You'll find that at some point in your life (perhaps already, I of course don't know) you become capable of moving through the entire passion of sexual stimulation and release without getting caught in the downside of sexual excitement. You simply surrender more and more to the heightened experience and erotic flow of your natural bodily desires and sexual programmings, right up to and through the total release of orgasm and bliss with your partner.

I raise the issue of excitement in this context of sexual love only because for most people, this positive rush of excitement also carries with it a most definitely negative rush as well, which I want to talk about, and explore how best to overcome. Sexual passion naturally alters our inner experience and our behaviour, moving us inexorably towards the body's desired genital union. Unfortunately for most of us, the movement towards sexual union also tends to push primary anxiety/uncertainty buttons, provoking an entire host of apprehensions and fears, inhibitions and contractions.

Even without any of our push-button fear-based reactions and inhibitions, approaching full sexual union with a partner carries immense significance because what we're approaching with our partner is nothing less than the ultimate creative act that human beings are capable of. Our sex drive carries as its primary intent, the merger of two beings sexually so that a new being can be created. We approach the role of playing God when we make love – we act out the archetypal creative act that lies at the heart of survival itself. We take on the definitely scary posture of creating out of seeming nothingness, a new living being who will carry on for us when we pass away, and ensure that human beings continue to populate this earth.

So definitely at the primordial level of sexual creation, the intensity and importance of our sexual act is amazing and exciting. If we make love and a new being is created, we've just accomplished perhaps our most important determining act of our lifetime. We've become a parent, and assumed the vast responsibilities of caring for our creation, creating a family, and maintaining a successful mate relationship hopefully until the baby is an adult.

Sure, we use contraceptives most of the time and hope that they work. And at some point we might have a simple operation and make ourselves sterile so that creation isn't an issue. And women at least attain freedom from the fear of unwanted pregnancy when they hit forty-five or so. But still our early apprehensions about pregnancy that we picked up as teenagers or in our twenties continue to influence how we feel when we make love. And deep down even if we don't intend to make a new baby when we make love, as we approach the passion of sexual abandon and release we awaken our primordial feelings of excitement about participating in the ultimate creative act of the human species.

The psychology of excitement when delved deeply into reveals that excitement almost always is a mixture of eager anticipation and uncertain apprehension. We become caught in the positive anticipation of experiencing something tremendously pleasurable coming our way as we approach a possible love mate – and at the same time, we all too often get caught in the negative apprehension that something seriously upsetting or dangerous or terrible might happen if we surrender to the crazy passion of sexual love.

If you look back to your early pubescent days, let's say from ten to twenty, you probably can remember any number of times when you got caught in terrible apprehensions and anxiety as you approached sexual excitement and possible release. Your breathing got tight with anxiety, you felt dizzy with apprehension, weak with fearful anticipation. The excitement of romance became inhibited by all your natural and culturally conditioned anxieties associated with sexual intimacy. Pause a few moments . . . close your eyes after reading this paragraph . . . tune into your breathing . . . and your heart . . . and begin to remember an experience when you were quite young, where the excitement of sexual arousal and passion caused an inner reaction of painful bashfulness and anxiety . . .

pause . . . breathe . . . reflect . . . experience

Intimacy and Excitement

Intimacy is such a powerful quality in relating. Successful sexual love requires that we not only take off our clothes and stand naked before another human being – we also must reveal our deeper emotions in order to attain fulfilling orgasm. At a certain point in genuine love-making (as opposed to casual sex) we actually move through a natural transformation where the dominance of our thinking controlling minds simply falls away, leaving us emotionally and spiritually naked as we approach orgasm.

This is what intimacy is all about – letting someone see us as we really are, naked in all ways. And this can be not only a most exhilarating positive experience, but also, if we're not prepared, a most frightening inhibiting predicament – which is why I have spent so much time already in this book, encouraging you to first of all tend your own inner garden, so that you know yourself well enough, and feel adequately positive about yourself, that you can indeed expose yourself to your new lover, and not feel ashamed or afraid of this act.

At a potent spiritual level it seems that as we approach the act of sexual creation, we've been designed so that we temporarily transcend our personal quirks and emotional contractions and so forth, and during the act of orgasm and creation, experience momentary transcendence and bliss, as if we for a few moments are in fact one with God and allowing the power of the Creator to flow freely through our mortal bodies, so that the new creation is a pure new being. If this is too esoteric for you, no matter – but I do feel that we've been created sexually in a most marvellous manner, so that at the moment of physical creation our own consciousness is pure and transcendent. That's why I find the experience of orgasm an utterly spiritual moment, when we do truly become one with God and know in our own hearts who we really are.

So certainly, sexual relating is exciting – we're asking to enter into a shared experience that not only carries the power to create new life, but also carries the power to temporarily transform our own lives, purify our souls, and awaken our contact with our true nature. In this light, it's clear why regular deep sexual relating can be so healthful and desired, even when creating a new being is entirely out of the picture. As the great sexual scientist Wilhelm Reich pointed out so clearly, sexual relating is our built-in assurance of, at least once or twice a week, entering into an experience that heals our emotions, cleanses our minds, invigorates our body, and awakens our sense of oneness with a higher order of consciousness and love.

You yourself are almost surely hungering for this transformational power of sexual union and release. Your animal drive for sexual union and your emotional need for intimacy and your spiritual yearning to feel temporarily one with another human being are all pushing you towards this most exciting and also quite scary encounter and experience that will come when you find your new lover.

Are you ready for this transformational experience that you hunger for? Are you prepared to put aside any old apprehensions, breathe into the rush of genuine excitement, and explore this level of intimacy with your chosen partner? Pause and focus inward . . . breath . . . heart . . . and actually feel your sexual yearning for the depths of healing and release that come with orgasm. Pause a few moments . . . allow your mind to become quiet . . . experience your excitement of anticipation . . . be open to a new experience.

pause . . . breathe . . . reflect . . . experience

Moderating The Rush

We are all addicts to the rush of sexual stimulation because when we become sexually excited, virtually every cell in our body becomes inundated with a complex hormonal cocktail that science has now identified as the orgasm compound. We're happily wired to crave this rush of whole-body transformation as each and every cell shifts its functioning and performance towards the orgasm experience. How blessed we are, compared to most other animals, to be programmed with this radically blissful pleasure response whenever we become sexually stimulated. Our challenge is to make sure we surrender to this bliss response only when appropriate, and without getting caught in the disrupting anxieties that often pollute the pure response with fearful thoughts and emotions, which in turn reduce our capacity to surrender to the rush of sexual pleasure.

What can you do to enjoy the sexual rush and, at the same time, minimize any fear reactions as you approach sexual relating? Let me teach you what works for me, and what you can readily adapt to your own life. You will want to return to this basic list often during the next days and weeks, if you tend to get overly excited and anxious when you turn your attention to finding and coming together with your new lover:

Excitement Control ONE: CHANGE YOUR BREATHING

The way in which you breathe moment to moment directly determines your charge of excitement. When you get excited you'll note that you tend to inhale a lot, hold on the inhale, and exhale shallowly. This breath pattern pushes loads of oxygen into your brain and body, which is fine if you go into action physically and burn that oxygen – as you do when actively making love. But if you start breathing excitedly long before you actually go into action sexually, this same way of breathing will make you dizzy, weak and uncomfortable. Fear is expressed as an inhale – you inhale when startled. Power and confidence are expressed as an exhale – you exhale slowly when you need to have power to push, for example.

The solution

To reduce feelings of anxiety when approaching love-making, exhales will be your best friend. Consciously begin to learn how to control your breathing, so that you purposely exhale deeply and 'hold' on empty at the bottom of your exhales . . . and inhale moderately without holding at the top of your inhale. And whenever you feel anxious or weak, develop the habit of focusing on your exhales so that you reduce your oxygen intake, and increase your sense of power deep-down in your belly.

Excitement Control TWO: IMPROVE YOUR SELF-IMAGE

Your underlying attitudes about your own sexuality can provoke unwanted excitement tinged with too much apprehension. We've worked a bit on this already, and you'll find that the basic attraction meditation will continue to stimulate new insights and emotional healing in this area. When you say to yourself, 'I love myself just as I am,' look carefully to see if you're accepting how you look, or if you're afraid you don't look good enough to attract your lover. Excitement quickly turns to apprehension when negative thoughts arise telling you that you're not sexy enough, and that you're going to be rejected when your desired encounter happens.

The solution

To overcome any ingrained attitudes and thoughts that sabotage your romantic hunt with apprehension, nervousness and worries, regularly spend time in meditation exploring your self-image as you did in an earlier chapter – and begin to improve your self-image so that you feel sexy and attractive, whatever body type you were born with. Become your own best friend so that whatever the outcome of your hunt, you continue to feel grounded solidly in your own love. And devote time to mastering the process of quieting your thoughts in general.

Excitement Control THREE: LET GO OF YOUR WORRIES

Excitement is not so much a function of the present moment, as it is a fixation on the future. All our worries, after all, come from imagining something bad happening to us in the future – anxiety is just that. A bad habit of the mind of regularly conjuring up fantasies of terrible things that might happen sometime in the future. Many people charge their bodies with negative excitement when they anticipate going out looking for their new love, by imagining all the bad things that could happen on that hunt. This is terribly self-defeating mental behaviour, and calls for definite mind management where you realize you're upsetting yourself with your thoughts, and choose instead to regain the present moment where your hunt can be both a pleasure, and a success.

The solution:

You've already begun working on this basic challenge of managing your mind so that you live more in the present moment, and less in the past and the future. The basic mental shifting process – where you direct your focus to your breathing, your heart, and your whole-body presence – will bring you away from upsetting thoughts, and into the relative bliss of the present moment. Your challenge when you feel shaky and tense with excitement about the future, is to remember to pull your attention back to the present moment, where you can regain your inner centre and proceed enjoyably on your hunt.

Excitement Control FOUR: STAY UNATTACHED TO OUTCOMES

As we saw in the previous chapter, when you become too fixated on outcomes, you generate uncertainty that makes you anxious with a negative charge of excitement. When you are demanding that a flow of events must move in the direction that your mind has previously decided is right, then you will become nervous and afraid when the flow of events doesn't unfold as you expect it to. The mental process of being attached to a particular image of how the future should unfold will generate negative excitement as you fearfully watch what's happening, and see reality unfolding differently from the outcome you're requiring.

The solution:

We're again in the realm of mind management – where you first of all observe your thoughts and catch yourself expecting the future to unfold according to your mind's projected outcome. When you see that you're doing this, you can choose to let go of your expectations of the future, and surrender to whatever comes. This is a required leap of faith in the hunt of the heart, where you trust life to unfold as it naturally will, and adapt your expectations to match reality. The key is to be content enough inside your own skin to the point where you're not feeling desperate to attain a particular outcome. And this contented feeling will come to you, through regularly doing the attraction meditation.

Surrendering To Passion

I suppose I'll be hollered at by some people for what I want to say at this point in our discussion, but here goes anyway. My feeling is that you will do better to regularly surrender to and engulf yourself in the excitement of sexual passion, than to try to control yourself and keep your excitement level low through self-denial. We've seen that your passion level determines your charge for attracting your lover to you. So obviously excitement is an important ingredient in our programme and not to be denied.

Excitement is a charge of energy in your body because of future expectations, that isn't getting released in the present moment. The problem with excitement isn't that there's too much of it, the problem is that the charge isn't being released creatively as you seek out your ultimate release. And the key question is this: how can you creatively release excess energy that keeps you too excited? Here are several excellent ways you can release your charge, so as to keep your energy level high but not bottled up inside you overlong:

• *Get Out and Dance*

As you know from experience, you actually have loads of surplus energy when you surrender to its flow through your body. I encourage you to regularly get out and dance. It doesn't matter where you do this as long as you feel safe and are having fun. You can also dance alone in your apartment or home. Feel your primal energies flowing in the dance, just as tribal societies have for countless generations. The discharge you experience while dancing with abandon can approximate the orgasmic discharge. No wonder dancing is so universally accepted and encouraged. Dance at least once a week if you can, while on the hunt.

• *Run Run Run*

Physical exercise of any kind will allow you to build up a powerful charge in your body, and discharge that energy in a beautiful way. You're aiming to make love with great passion with your new lover – and making love is a physical sport just as much as cycling or tennis or any other sport is. The better shape you're in, the bigger your charge will be while making love. So one way or another, be it a daily brisk walk or a game of football or a swim in the local pool – get out and get moving to where your heart pounds and your breaths become powerful. In the process, you'll also find that your self-image improves, your sexiness is enhanced, and your overall sense of power and presence accentuated. Do it!

• *Enjoy Fantasy Breaks*

To encourage the flow of passion through your whole being, I recommend regular fantasy breaks in which you sit or lie down for five to ten minutes, perhaps before drifting off to sleep, after a meal or whenever you want, and indulge in a totally uninhibited daydream of a romantic encounter. Play out all your various notions of what might happen to you with your new love. Be entirely unjudgmental about what you fantasize, so you can discover your own hidden and sometimes mostly buried depths of desire and pleasure. Begin to accept yourself as a wild sexual animal, even as you accept yourself as a blissful spiritual being. Bringing the two together is what makes sexual relating so illuminating.

• *Give Yourself Pleasure*
Beyond all the cultural inhibitions and religious restrictions on self-pleasure, almost everyone in the world does it and enjoys it. If we're to truly be our own best friend, and there's no one else to help us feel good sexually, it makes perfect psychological sense to help ourselves – doesn't it? Research has proven that masturbation (without guilt feelings) is definitely a healthy psychological experience unless it becomes compulsive. And it won't become compulsive if you're doing your attraction meditations and taking yourself out hunting regularly for a real-life lover. As a preparation for deep sexual relating, masturbation prepares you to let go and surrender to the rush of orgasmic pleasure and release. You get to know yourself and understand how sexual energy flows. And then when you do come together with your lover, you're ready both to understand your lover's sexual needs, and yours as well. Let's put away all the 'dirty' notions of masturbation, and employ this universal self-pleasure routine as a temporary stand-in for the real thing. You're going to come in your sleep if you don't when awake – so you'd might as well consciously participate in the process.

IMAGINING THE ENCOUNTER

We've now built right up to the point where you have the tools to take you to the moment of encounter with your new love. Of course you'll probably want to return to the beginning and spend more time on your preparations on all fronts. Who knows, maybe you'll put this book down today, look up – and there will be your dream love standing in front of you, gazing with recognition into your eyes . . . and perhaps on the other hand you'll continue alone and preparing for days, weeks, months . . . this is the mystery.

Meanwhile let me share with you a special preparation you can do every day if you want to, to prepare for new encounter, and see how ready you are for love, and where you might need more preparation. Each time you move through this fantasy meditation, please be open to a new experience – and with each new fantasy experience, allow insight to come, healing to happen, and love to flow. This meditation and the others in this chapter can be explored in much more depth online, and in my book and CDs called 'Sex and Spirit'.

Make yourself comfortable . . . let your attention turn to your breathing . . . stretch and yawn if you want to . . . feel the air flowing in and out your nose . . . expand to feel the movements in your chest and belly as you breathe . . . and open up to experience the feelings in your heart right now, as you begin to turn your attention towards your yearnings for sexual love . . .

As your breaths come and go without any effort, begin to imagine that you're out someplace . . . walking around . . . or sitting someplace . . . see where you'd like to be right now, and imagine being there, doing whatever pleases you . . . allow yourself to feel good inside your own body . . . your breathing is free . . . you're content inside your own skin . . . and at the same time, you're observing the world around you, attentive as always to perhaps suddenly encountering your new lover . . .

You feel sexy in your body . . . you like yourself just as you are . . . there's plenty of love flowing . . . you're open to whatever happens . . . life is good . . . and as you continue to let time go by, to move as you want to . . . suddenly you find yourself looking at a person . . . and that person looks at you . . . and your eyes look away – then back again. You feel your breathing tense with excitement . . . all thoughts drop away . . . your jaw drops . . . your breathing momentarily seems lost . . . there's nothing but you – and this person looking at you . . .

And now see what happens, as your imagination takes you into action, and your long-awaited encounter begins to unfold . . . let it happen . . . enjoy the experience – stay with your own centre, and enter into relaxed and at the same time excited new relating . . .

pause . . . breathe . . . reflect . . . experience

Chapter 12

Discovering Each Other

Yes! Unless the good Lord wills otherwise, you are headed directly towards manifesting your dream, and coming face to face with the new love of your life. When this happens is likewise to be determined by forces beyond your control – but your intent and willpower, your yearning and preparations, your active broadcasting and receiving, are all strongly tilting fate in your favour. In this chapter I'd like to talk about the moment of actual encounter, and the moments following. Then in the next short section we'll explore pragmatic ways to ensure that the new relationship flourishes in accordance with its natural evolution.

Last night I lay in bed reflecting upon writing this special chapter about the actual moment of your encounter with someone who will be very special in your life. In doing so, I allowed my mind to vividly remember each of the most important and beautiful relationships I've been blessed with this lifetime. I encourage you to do the same – relive all the deep heart encounters you've already had, explore how they happened, how you reacted, how you were touched by the relationship, and the outcome of that encounter in your life, in the long run.

What I realize so clearly now, is that new love can come into our hearts only when we have prepared a space in our hearts for new love. So many lonely people are lonely specifically because even though they yearn almost tragically for someone to come into their lives, they have yet to open up free space in their hearts for someone to live. In a very real sense, when we fall in love, we welcome that new person into our hearts. And for space to exist in our hearts for a new person, certain things need to happen.

Primarily, during the attraction meditation, you will need to spend plenty of time with your mind quiet, and focused on your heart. As I've taught you, it's vitally important to hold the presence of your new lover in your heart – and to do this, you must dedicate space in your heart to this person. There must be open free available loving room in your heart. Only then can love at first sight happen – because what really happens in that moment of eye-heart-soul encounter is that both of you suddenly find yourselves welcomed right into the other's heart. Suddenly you're connected through the deepest of energetic links, heart to heart.

I differentiate my love life based on the following: there are a great many people with whom I've been friendly over the years – and there are a relatively small number where something more permanent happened. When I have truly fallen in love, or recognized a true brother or sister and entered into a deep friendship, this special feeling of being in that other person's heart and having their loving presence in my heart never leaves me. I can think of this person even if I haven't seen them for forty years, and instantly feel them in my heart. True love is indeed eternal at this level – and this is what makes love so amazing. It definitely transcends space and time, and continues throughout our lives.

I remember in this light, the first girl who stole my heart, as we say. I was eleven, at a church camp, and in the swimming pool. I was a shy boy but at the same time, that summer I felt a powerful new feeling of yearning in my heart – the primordial aching for an ideal romantic love. This feeling that comes with puberty, or even before for many people, clearly has a genetic instinctual dimension, and also a cultural psychological dimension, and surely a pure spiritual dimension as well. With zero anticipation I remember turning my head and suddenly meeting the soft blue eyes of a blond-haired girl about forty feet away from me – and pow! I was knocked flat, I couldn't breathe – something happened to me for the first time that almost made me pass out.

We stared at each other, lost to space and time . . . until someone banged into me and she disappeared. I saw her again at dinner across the room, and was so shy I could hardly bring myself to meet her eyes. She was likewise very shy and the whole week passed without our even saying a single word to each other, even though we were consumed with each other. I never saw this girl again, and yet she continues to live in my heart so strongly that I spend a few minutes probably once a week, just feeling her in my heart, wherever she is . . . she's a part of me.

> You surely had a similar moment of first heart encounter – what happened, and how do you feel about that first love of your life, even if the love wasn't in any way acted upon like mine . . . does this person still live in your heart? Take some time to remember . . . relive . . . and feel this person in your heart . . .

pause . . . breathe . . . reflect . . . experience

Teen Love

As mentioned before, we encounter many people who strike us strongly, even if they don't end up being a lover or long-term mate. There are a great many people with whom we're compatible, but whose lives are flowing in different directions than ours are, so that we perhaps look in their eyes and recognize a kindred spirit, but that's it – no further opportunity to explore a relationship. This especially happens in our teen years, where romance flashes here and there, sometimes developing into going steady but usually not being acted upon at all.

During our teen years we often fixate our loving attention on unattainable heart-throbs such as pop music stars, movie actors, a teacher who just overwhelms our hearts without even meaning to – and other students who for one reason or another don't pay us any attention. These early romances and heartbreaks can feel devastating, and deeply wound us as we mature and explore sexual relating. I remember a girl in seventh grade who totally stole my heart with her casual big-eye glances, but who never seemed to have any romantic interest in me. For a year I was wildly in love with her and her alone, but nothing ever came of it. Still, even though she didn't take me much into her heart, I took her into mine, and she's still there like a pure light, the look in her eye setting me afire with the simple yet extremely intense passion of teen love.

I also remember girls who wanted to be my girlfriend, but whom I didn't respond to sexually. Yes, we do break other people's hearts, and often there's nothing that can be done about it, no blame – just the confusion of disjointed attraction. When we find someone who wakes us up sexually and on deeper spiritual levels, but who never responds likewise to us, there comes a time when it's essential to pull our love back, and open our hearts to finding a new person where the attraction is mutual. Sometimes we have to assert our power to make a decision heart-wise, and demand that our hearts listen to our reason about a relationship. This can be difficult, but in the attraction meditation, you'll find that you can find a quiet place in your heart, and open space to a new love who will give you what you yearn for – this is your act of intent that changes your life and opens you to new experience.

What was your love life like back in high school . . . take a few moments to pause . . . let memories come . . . relive the moments of encounter that were short flashes in your romantic unfolding . . . and moments of encounter that perhaps developed into longer relationships. Be honest, see who you took into your heart, and feel if you have these people still in your heart . . .

pause . . . breathe . . . reflect . . . experience

Lovers Coming . . . And Going

I was a senior in college at Princeton, which back then was an all-men's university. Most of the time life was pretty lonely romance-wise. And the girl I thought I had a date with that weekend cancelled. Out of the blue my roommate found out his sister was coming into town with her friend from Seattle, and he asked me if I'd be nice enough to take a blind date with her. I remember the moment when I decided to say yes to that offer. I'd had terrible experiences with blind dates, and I'd already decided to go into New York to a play I wanted to see. My logical mind said no – but I found my mouth saying yes.

The next afternoon I found myself shaking hands with a most wonderful girl, looking into her eyes – and being hit with love at first sight. We were instantly in each other's hearts and moved through a wild love affair that ended in marriage and the birth of my first son. And even though a few years later the relationship simply blew up in our faces because in so many ways we were so very different and headed in entirely divergent directions, that love of course remains eternally in my heart.

Perhaps the most intense spiritual affair of my life happened as if fate refused to take no for an answer. I'd met a woman while my son and I were living in my hometown of Ojai, California. Her daughter and my son went to the same little school, so I often talked with this lovely woman – but we both were engaged in other relationships at the time. There was no great spark when we looked in each other's eyes, and when work took me to another state, there was no sense of loss in leaving her. She was just a person among many persons whom I felt friendly with, but nothing more.

Then a series of quite unexpected events led me back to Ojai a year or so later. I don't think I'd even thought of this woman in the interim, and I was standing in line at the bank to open an account, turned around casually – and there she was right behind me. And again, pow! We were both so overwhelmed that we couldn't even find words to talk for the entire time we stood in line – we just looked in each other's eyes. And from that moment there was no question, we were head over heels in love in a most passionate relationship that seemed destined to be a lifetime affair. She took me into realms of consciousness I never dreamed existed, and healed old heart wounds I didn't even know I had. Our love was eternal and on fire – and then nine months later suddenly the passion changed, events and needs pulled us apart, and that was that. Except for the blessed fact that we are still in each other's hearts and always will be.

I tell these rather personal accounts because I feel it so important to emphasize that even love affairs that don't continue forever, continue to nurture us if we allow the other person to live within our hearts. We can't do anything about the manoeuvrings of fate which determine if we stay with someone forever or for a short time – but we can continue to hold love in our hearts for those who have been close with us physically in the past. And each time we fall in love, if we're unattached to outcomes, and truly love without possessing the other person, we gain a gift from that person that is essential to our spiritual and romantic evolution. Even when we happen to get on the subway and suddenly stare into the eyes of another person and experience just ten seconds of total oneness and attraction – and then never see that person again – we've received the eternal gift of being touched in the heart with love. And that's what life is all about – sharing love, letting people feel our love in our hearts . . . and allowing life to unfold as it will.

We can only be strong enough to let love come and go without trying to attach ourselves to a particular bearer of that love, if we have done our heart preparations and become our own best friend. This is why I continue to mention how important it is to do a daily meditation in which you nurture your love and acceptance for your own self, so that you go out into the world feeling satisfied inside your own heart, even before you fall in love. You can feel whole as an individual, and still open your heart to love. As I said before, it's a two hundred per cent world – you can be a hundred percent whole on your own, and offer a hundred per cent of yourself to another person. That's the dynamic of mature unconditional love.

Take some time right now to reflect upon your progress in becoming your own best friend. Are you ready to let someone new into your heart, and still remain unattached to the outcome of the affair? Can you share love in the present moment without feeling the fear of losing that love in the future? Are you ready to enter into a new sexual partnership where trust and faith sustain the relationship, and the promise of eternal friendship sets you both free to let the relationship evolve as it naturally will? Take some time to breathe . . . tune into your heart . . . and see what insights and inner experiences come to you now . . .

pause . . . breathe . . . reflect . . . experience

The Mating Instinct

Now that we've fully discussed the importance of being unattached to outcomes in your new relationship, I want to equally focus on the opposite – that even though most people move through several or even ten or twenty shorter-term sexual relationships before finding their long-term sexual mate, our natural instinct does push us towards finding a person with whom we can settle in, live the rest of our life, and perhaps have children.

In your daily attraction meditation, you will regularly reflect upon what kind of relationship your heart is yearning for right now. Are you still in the exploratory stage, enjoying dating and romance but not ready for a long-term or permanent relationship? Or have you reached the point where you no longer have time for temporary romance that comes and goes – are you now determined to find that lifelong mate?

When my own second marriage came to an amicable but inevitable end, I was thirty-two and still a wild young guy. I spent a couple years travelling, living with native tribes doing research, pounding nails on a couple houses, working at the family ranch and in general, enjoying being single again and on the move. But then something happened – for the first time, I felt a new type of romantic yearning in my heart. I was no longer all that interested in what I began to see as shallow romance. A new desire began to grow in me – that of settling down with one woman for the rest of my life.

For several months I couldn't quite believe what I was feeling. I was forced first of all to admit that until that point in my life, I hadn't really been ready for the role of father and long-term mate. I'd been a kid even in my late twenties, and even though I'd jumped into two marriages, I hadn't really been ready for that level of devotion. During my daily reflections and meditations, I quietly looked inward and let go of my self-image as a young independent fun guy, and began to discover a new identity emerging, in which I felt more mature, ready for the experience of being a father and provider, and uninterested in women who weren't also beginning to commit to the mating instinct.

To punctuate my growing feeling of having moved into a new period of my life, I moved to Europe and started working in West Berlin, and travelling to five other cities doing weekend seminars and training groups. Yes, there was considerable romance in the air and I met a number of wonderful women with whom the flash of recognition happened. But more and more I was becoming clear in my heart that my intent was to remain quite single, until I found that very special woman with whom I'd want to have children and live the rest of my life, God willing of course.

I have no idea if you're at this stage of your life where your yearning is towards finding someone to start a family with and live with the rest of your life. You'll know in your meditations – and if you are intent upon this level of new romance, then quite naturally you'll broadcast this serious intent out to the world, and attract a like-minded person into your arms. This means that even though you might meet other people with whom the flash of romantic recognition happens, you're not responding to that flash until you feel you've found someone who resonates with your deeper desire for a permanent mate. To be honest is what's most important here. Honest with yourself, and honest with those you meet. The truth will set you free, as always.

Pause a few moments to tune into your breathing . . . your feelings
. . . and reflect upon the kind of relationship you want to bring
into being. Are you enjoying being adventuresome and romantic
without necessarily wanting to settle into a long-term relationship, or are you feeling ready for a long-term and perhaps if you're
lucky, life-long mating experience?

pause . . . breathe . . . reflect . . . experience

Here It Comes!

Whatever you are seeking in your new relationship, we're now at the
point where you surrender to it happening in your life. You are advancing towards establishing and maintaining your daily attraction
meditation. You're remembering many times a day to pause and tune
into your yearnings and intent romantically. You're developing the fine
art of being on the hunt of the heart wherever you go, so that you're
awake and ready in the present moment for that unexpected fateful
encounter. And you're managing your excitement so that your attractive charge is high without being stressed or anxious. You're step by
step taking fate in your own hands by preparing yourself for true love,
and actively seeking it. You're also learning in your meditation experience to tap into your greater wisdom and guidance, so that you
surrender to and participate in the higher spiritual process that brings
true hearts together.

It all comes down to this – right now, there is someone out there
who is destined to suddenly look in your eyes and recognize you as a
kindred spirit, as their next and perhaps ultimate lover. They are out
there looking for you – and you are right here, open to find them. This
is exciting, and it's real, and it's happening. You're going to suddenly
discover each other. You're going to transform each other's lives with
your love and presence. You're going to dance the mating game, and
perhaps even create a new being together.

And right in the middle of all this exciting adventure of the hunt of the heart, you're also learning how to be calm and centred within your own heart and soul. You're discovering how to have faith, and to surrender to the higher will. You're managing your mind so that you aren't needy nor grabby nor lonely on your own. This is a challenge, and you are working to master it. You don't want a lover who's a wreck emotionally. You don't want a partner who fearfully attaches to your heart. You don't want a friend who doesn't know how to give you space in their heart – so you know that you need to likewise prepare your own heart and soul so that you're ready for an emotionally and spiritually healthy relationship. I've sung this song for you enough so that I'm sure you now know it by heart, and I'll now become quiet in this regard, and trust that you will assume full responsibility for carrying on . . . great!

And so we end this second part of this book focused on the hunt of the heart, and move on to a short discussion of things you can do to ensure that when you do come together with a new lover, you optimize your chances of a fulfilling relationship and inner growth and sharing.

To end this chapter, let's return to the beginning – to your inner feeling of being attractive, and ready to let love find you. Everything depends on how you feel in your own heart. You are the manager of your heart and mind, and I've given you the mental tools that will enable you to aim your mind's power of attention in the directions most effective in generating the results you dearly desire.

So let's move through the basic attraction meditation again here, so that you remember what's come before, and see how this daily meditation process directly aims your whole being towards succeeding in the hunt of the heart. Read through the full process, pausing to experience each step – and remember that there's also online audio guidance to help you memorize the process.

FULL ATTRACTION MEDITATION

Find a quiet time and place where you can enjoy the bliss and empowerment of entering the deep state of harmony found in this meditation. Set aside fifteen to forty-five minutes when you have plenty of time to relax . . . Remember that nurturing the feeling of effortless joy is the key inner quality to encourage here . . . no pushing, just enjoyable exploration, with a new experience coming to you each time:

◆ Make sure you're feeling comfortable in your body – feel free to stretch all you want, and yawn . . . let your body move as it wants to, to discharge tensions.

◆ Tune into the air flowing in and out your nose (or mouth) as you breathe . . . expand your awareness to include the movements in your chest and belly as your breaths come and go and come again . . . and gently expand your awareness to include the feelings in your heart, right in the middle of your breathing.

◆ Accept whatever feelings you find right now, breathe into them, let them change with each new breath . . .

◆ Expand your awareness to include your whole body, here in this present moment. Be aware of your toes . . . your hands . . . your throat . . . your pelvis . . . your knees . . . your belly . . . allow your awareness to move around your body and find places that feel especially good right now . . . enjoy the good feelings you find . . . move all you want to let these good feelings expand . . .

◆ Bring your focus to your breathing again . . . open more to the feelings in your heart . . . and begin to think of someone in your life whom you love. Let your love for this person fill your heart as you aim your attention towards this person, wherever they may be – they will feel your attention when you aim it towards them . . . they can feel your love . . . enjoy this heart-to-heart communion . . .

◆ And now you can shift into receive mode in your heart, so that you begin to feel the love this person has for you . . . open your heart, and let their love come in . . .

◆ And open your heart more as you let all the pure spiritual love of the universe come flowing into your heart . . . with every new breath, be open to receive more love, until your whole heart and

being fills with love . . . relax and enjoy this vibrant loving
feeling . . .

◆ And now, gently return your attention to your breaths, coming and
going . . . and begin to say the following focus phrases that will
awaken new experience in your heart, mind and soul . . .

1. Yearning

The feelings in your heart are the power you have to heal . . . to reach
out . . . to manifest your lover . . . after saying each of these focus
phrases, pause and see how you feel in your heart, about the intent
you just stated:

'I want to heal my emotional wounds . . .'
'I feel a deep yearning for new love . . .'
'I am going to attract new love to me . . .'

~ pause & experience ~

2. Forgiving and Healing

It's time to let go . . . to accept . . . to forgive . . . and to open up and
receive healing and love . . . say the intent . . . experience the
reverberations of the words . . .

'I accept and love myself, just as I am.'
'I forgive and let go of my old lovers.'
'My heart is open to receive . . . healing . . . and love.'

~ pause & experience ~

3. Waking Up Sexually

You are as beautiful as you feel inside . . . let yourself feel good . . . let
the world see you as attractive and powerful and full of love . . .

'I am a beautiful powerful sexual being.'
'I give myself permission to feel good in my body.'
'See me – sexually attractive . . . ready for love.'

~ pause & experience ~

4. Charging

Now let's focus specifically on the passion you feel inside your body, in your heart, in your belly, in your genitals, in your throat – in your whole body. Say the statements one by one, breathe . . . and pause to experience whatever new feelings and insights come to you . . .

'I feel passion . . . in my heart . . . in my belly. . .'

'I feel sexual hunger in my genitals . . . in my throat . . .'

'My whole being is charged with loving energy.'

~ pause & experience ~

5. Broadcasting

It's time to let the world know you're here and you're ready for your true love. Say it – do it! Let these words empower you . . . wake up the world to your desire . . . and aim your intent directly towards that person out there who is also aiming towards you . . .

'Here I am right now, yearning for love.'

'I am reaching out to you . . .'

'Feel me . . . come into my life.'

~ pause & experience ~

6. Surrendering

Now let's move deeper . . . allow your thoughts to become quiet . . . your breathing even and deep . . . and go ahead and ask for help and guidance . . . open your entire being to the greater loving force that will bring your heart together with your lover-to-be . . .

'My mind is quiet . . . my breathing calm.'

'I request help from my deeper source.'

'I surrender to spiritual wisdom and guidance.'

~ pause & experience ~

7. Moving Towards Encounter

And now go all the way . . . open up to experience connection with your lover . . . say it . . . experience it . . . from the depths of your heart, say the following statements . . . pause after each one . . . breathe . . . experience . . .

'I let go of inhibitions . . .'
'I need you . . . I love you . . .'
'Here I am – I feel you!'

~ pause & experience ~

◆ And now you can just relax . . . stay with your feelings . . . allow your breaths to deepen . . . and as you hold your heart open to your new lover, feel in your whole body what this person is like . . . as if you are already in your lover's arms . . . look deeply into your lover's eyes . . . see your lover's soul . . . and feel how you are together already in spirit . . .

◆ You can stay in meditation for as long as you want . . . and when you're ready you can open your eyes . . . stretch and yawn . . . and as you go about your day, be spontaneous in where you go . . . so that your two bodies can move closer and closer towards each other . . . let spirit move you through your day . . . as you come closer to suddenly encountering each other . . . looking into each other's eyes . . . and knowing – that you have found your true love!

pause . . . breathe . . . reflect . . . experience

Part Three:

NURTURING YOUR NEW LOVE LIFE

Chapter 13

Your

Independent

Centre

R ight at the moment that you do meet someone new who wakes you up and turns you on, you have a great challenge that will determine much of what happens as that new relationship develops. We talked before about the vast difference between puppy love and co-dependent attachment, and mature love where you hold on to your independent centre even while enjoying deep sharing and sexual oneness with this new person. It's the difference between regressing backwards into feelings and actions appropriate for a young child, and advancing forward into feelings and actions appropriate for your adult status.

I don't mean to sound judgmental here, or in any way harsh about puppy love. We all move through that phase in life. What I'm encouraging is your realization that it's to your advantage not to regress into feelings that will make you cling to your new love, for fear of losing your own centre. As long as you simply set your intent clearly, to maintain your own independent centre in your own heart, you can plunge totally into sexual passion and deep love emotions.

What's key here is observing the thoughts that arise when you do fall in love. Notice if you're starting to think the thought, 'I can't live without this person,' for instance. And if you do find yourself saying such things to yourself, and feeling the resulting emotions of fear of losing your lover, you can directly counter these thoughts and feelings by asking yourself the following: 'Is it true that I can't live without this person in my life?'

Yes, this person makes you feel very good and fills your life with wonderful experiences. Yes, this person helps you feel complete and satisfied – but if you have maintained your sense of being your own best friend, you know that you can indeed live and survive and even thrive, on your own. This person is not your mother and you are not a dependent child. You are an independent adult, and there are many people out there who can come together with you to fulfil your romantic yearnings.

The good news is this. If you're ready for a mature relationship between adults, the person you've attracted to you, and whom you're attracted to, probably feels basically the same as you do. Early on in your relationship, you'll want to openly talk about this issue. Express your new feelings of wanting to share a love that's not possessive – this is key! Make sure that this person you're beginning to relate deeply with shares your own attitudes about the kind of relationship you want. And if they don't, be strong enough to walk away from the relationship. Be your own best friend in this regard – choose to relate deeply with people who share your underlying yearnings for a mature relationship.

Relationships work best where both participants share similar views on most important issues in life. If you find that you're with someone who wants you to think differently than you do, behave differently than you do, and relate differently than you do, don't become overly involved with this person because you're liable to lose your own centre and sense of who you are, by trying to please this person. I know this can be hard, but I'm wanting to talk reality.

As you enter into the hunt of the heart, there will probably come a number of opportunities for romance. You've prepared yourself for love, you're ready – so you'll be attractive. This means you can indeed pick and choose, and take your time to explore a number of different people to whom you're attracted. Because through doing the preparations we've been talking about, you already love yourself and feel good inside your own skin; you're free to relax even in the heat of passion, step back into your own private awareness and evaluate what's happening in your new love affair.

Again, the good news is that if you assert your individual right to hold your own centre, and be your own best friend, you're probably going to attract someone who feels the same way – and you're going to enjoy the thrill of exploring life and love with someone who's on the same path as you are. If you're regularly retreating and reflecting even as the new love relationship begins, you can decide if you should plunge deeper, or pull back from the emerging relationship.

Continuing With Your Meditation Practice

Finding your true love should be seen as the beginning, not the end, of your inner process of personal reflection and successful mind management. Negotiating the sometimes placid, sometimes wild waters of a sexual involvement can be vastly easier and more enjoyable when you maintain your daily routine of retreating for half an hour, or even ten minutes if that's all you can manage, to tune inward, look to your heart, and contact your deeper source of wisdom, guidance and love.

So I encourage you strongly to make sure your daily routine of private retreat into quiet meditation doesn't fall aside, when the passion of having found your lover takes over your life. The simple act of retreating for half an hour a day will indicate clearly to your partner that you value your own centre, that you take ongoing responsibility for nurturing your inner spiritual growth and emotional healing. If you find yourself with a partner who doesn't respect your need and desire to enter into quiet reflection once a day, then of course you should reflect upon whether you're with the right person after all.

And the same goes, the other way around. Be sure to grant your new friend private retreat time. When two lovers cling to each other constantly and don't separate regularly to catch their separate breaths, the relationship tends to suffocate and die. When two lovers regularly retreat from each other into their own separate lives, breathing space is created that directly nurtures the relationship.

Here's the curious thing that all too often happens when people fall wildly in love. They of course are in love with the uniqueness of their lover. But as time goes by, if that uniqueness isn't nurtured, if the two hearts and personalities get lost somewhere in the middle of the two separate centres, at some point the passion will fail because the polarity between two separate individuals has been lost. If you want to maintain a long-term relationship, I strongly advise making sure that you nurture your own separate personal presence and charge, through meditation and other activities separate from the other person.

This regular retreat away from the other person will enable both of you to recharge, so that when you come back together, there's a new flash of attraction. Especially in meditation, you'll find that you can quickly recharge your emotional energy through pausing, tuning into your breathing . . . and dwelling at peace in your own inner centre. As you reconnect with your higher wisdom and creative source, you'll make sure that you remain attractive . . . and the relationship will thrive.

Relationship Meditation

Let me present you with a simple meditation, combining the meditation you've learned with new dimensions, to serve you as support for your new relationship when it happens. Hold in mind that this exploration of how to negotiate a successful relationship is a vast discussion, and we're only touching on the essentials here:

Make sure you're feeling comfortable in your body – feel free to stretch all you want, and yawn . . . let your body move as it wants to, to discharge tensions. Tune into the air flowing in and out your nose . . . expand your awareness to include the movements in your chest and belly as you breathe . . . and gently expand your awareness to include the feelings in your heart, right in the middle of your breathing. Accept whatever feelings you find right now, breathe into them, let them change with each new breath . . .

Expand your awareness to include your whole body, here in this present moment. Be aware of your toes . . . your hands . . . your throat . . . your pelvis . . . your knees . . . your belly . . . allow your awareness to move around your body and find places that feel especially good right now . . . enjoy the good feelings you find . . . move all you want to let these good feelings expand . . .

Bring your focus to your breathing again . . . open more to the feelings in your heart . . . and begin to think of someone in your life whom you love. Let your love for this person fill your heart as you aim your attention towards this person, wherever they may be – they will feel your attention when you aim it towards them . . . they can feel your love . . . enjoy this heart-to-heart communion . . .

And now you can shift into receive mode in your heart, so that you begin to feel the love this person has for you . . . open your heart, and let their love come in . . .

And now open your heart more . . . and allow all the pure spiritual love of the universe to come flowing into your heart . . . with every new breath, be open to receive more love, until your whole heart and being fills with love . . . relax and enjoy this vibrant loving feeling . . .

And now, gently return your attention to your breaths, coming and going . . . and begin to say the following focus phrases that will awaken new experience in your heart, mind and soul . . .

'I am ready to let old emotional wounds heal.'

'I accept and love myself, just as I am.'

'My heart is open to receive emotional healing . . . and love.'

'I am a beautiful powerful sexual being.'

'I am open to guidance from my deeper spiritual source.'

'I can be happy without my lover, if I so choose.'

'I accept who my lover is, without any judgment.'

'I let go of inhibitions . . . I'm open to passion and love.'

And now you can just relax . . . stay with your feelings . . . allow your breaths to come and go, without any effort at all . . . and hold your heart open to your lover . . . and as you explore your new relationship, continue to hold and nurture your own inner centre, as you also open yourself to deep, loving and joyful union.

You can stay in meditation as long as you want to . . . and when you're ready you can open your eyes . . . stretch and yawn .. and carry on with your day.

pause . . . breathe . . . reflect . . . experience

Chapter 14:

Love That's Free To Flourish

When you come together with another human being, and enter into the most intimate of relationships, you can either allow your cultural and childhood programmings about sexual relating to dictate what you do and how your relationship advances, or you can choose together to consciously create your own unique relationship based on the guidance of your inner wisdom and the new love inflowing into your hearts. Something new does come into being when two human beings come together in sexual love. Even if you don't create a new physical being and start a family, the two of you together become a unique loving force in the universe, where the merger of your energies empowers you to act together in ways you never would have acted separately.

I so highly honour conscious relationships, where both partners realize that they have come together for some higher purpose, and that together they are exploring new realms of love and creativity. Yes, we do need to maintain our separate centres, as mentioned in the previous chapter. But at the same time in this two hundred per cent universe we live within, at a certain level we do merge our hearts and souls to form something new, something powerful, something grounded entirely in the universal power and wisdom of spiritual love.

I've written several books about 'sex and spirit' and 'kundalini awakening' and so forth because for me, the merger of sex and spirit is what life is all about. Our carnal sexual drives and actions are not opposites to our ephemeral spiritual yearnings and realizations. The very act of being created by our parents as a new physical being is our initiation into the merger of sex and spirit. And as we mature and enter into sexual relationships, we enter into a vast exploration of who we are sexually and spiritually, and in the act of orgasm experience the two exploding into one greater reality.

Our greatest challenge seems to be learning how to love someone completely, and at the same time, to let that person be entirely free to lead their life as spirit moves them. Nothing kills passion faster than possessiveness, and nothing unleashes infinite passion like freedom does. Even though we might feel totally one with our love while making love, as our personal identities drop away and our universal identities come to the fore, when we're not making love, it's vital to continually recognize the uniqueness of our lover, rather than trying to become the same with no differences.

And if we're to truly nurture the unfolding life of the one we love, we must set that person entirely free so that they can grow and unfold without feeling caught in our concept of who they should be and what they should do. That's what Birgitta and I have found – that through founding our relationship on the total freedom of the other person to come and go as they are so moved, our relationship has endured twenty-some years without even once our feeling that the other person was going to desert us. When we have the freedom to leave the other person, we experience such a powerful blessing and bliss as we find that spirit holds us naturally together.

Natural Mates

I firmly believe that it is our inherent human nature to seek for and find someone to spend our lives with. This is the foundation of family after all, and without family, there is no human race, period. Yes, we also have a dimension of us that remains stuck in the hunt of the heart even after we've won the hunt. Our teenage singles hunting habits often kick into gear even after we've found our true love. We do have the tendency to want to be single again and caught up in the rush of sexual adventure and so forth. However, the yearning to find and stay with a mate for life is very strong.

The remarkable pay-off to staying in a loving relationship for many years is that every year, that relationship matures, new challenges and discoveries emerge, and the depth of the relationship continues to reach new realms of intimacy. Sometimes I hear people complaining about how boring their marriage has become, but I can't quite fathom that feeling. The only thing that makes staying with the same lover boring is when you don't feel free in that relationship. Each of us is an infinite spiritual being. When we're free to explore our infinite realms of consciousness, we are definitely not boring to our long-term mate. I still have no idea who Birgitta is, she's more and more a mystery to me, as we explore together our spiritual depths. And it's such a remarkable blessing, to be able to explore life together with someone, rather than alone. When a relationship is seen in this light, love flourishes!

Pause a moment after reading this paragraph, close your eyes if you want to . . . and let yourself imagine what it might be like, to spend the rest of your life with a deep loving partner who's as open to exploring life and love as you are . . . reflect on whether this is something that you yearn for, the breadth of love and discovery that comes only from being with the same person through one experience after another, year after year . . .

pause . . . breathe . . . reflect . . . experience

Chapter 15:

Your Hearts Singing Together

There has been overmuch talk about how hard couples must work, in order to have a successful relationship. In my marriage counselling work I actually advise just the opposite. Don't believe that you have to work hard and struggle continually, in order to live together harmoniously. Instead, as we've been learning, you can master the mind-management process of loving your partner just as they are, rather than demanding that they change before you love them.

When we become close with someone, we tend to start sticking our noses into their business. Because we're so close, some of their differences begin to bother us – and so we think they should change how they are, so as not to bother us. Likewise when we let someone get very close to us in all ways, our personal habits and attitudes can begin to bother them. This is where marriage counsellors often come in, and help the two members of a marriage struggle to change how they are, so that the marriage will be harmonious.

I have a very different approach that seems to work much better to encourage lasting love. If you're so close to your lover that who you are is bothering them, just back off until the distance is right, to get along. As I mentioned before, one of the main causes of death for relationships is by smothering. We think that true love means being very close all the time in all ways – but that's just not the reality of a lasting relationship.

In contrast, all successful relationships are based on a regular pulsation, where sometimes you're very close to your partner emotionally, and sometimes quite distant. Holding on to each other too tightly always stifles a relationship. Rather, couples need to learn to practise the fine art of 'successful distancing' in which the pulsation of coming very close, then letting go and moving somewhat apart, is respected and encouraged.

Two hearts can joyfully sing together for a lifetime when this freedom to move temporarily apart is included in the basic dynamic of the relationship. When both members of the relationship are quite happy alone because they love themselves as much as they love their partner, a healthy heart condition exists which allows for regular distancing, which in turn encourages long-term friendship and lifelong mating. Caged birds don't sing, at least not as much as free birds. And when we let our lover be truly free, without worried jealous attachments, then two hearts can remain together forever.

What do you think of this notion of not constantly holding on and being close to your new lover when he or she appears? What are you actually wanting now – the closeness you had with your mother, that total loss of self in another's love? Or are you wanting to learn the dynamics that sustain long-term relationships and still keep the passion aflame? I know these might be new ideas for you, and I also know we can only touch them briefly here at the end of our 'finding each other' programme. I just want to start your mind and heart reflecting on these vital issues that will influence how your new relationship evolves – check out online discussions for more.

Take a minute or two now if you want to, to put the book aside, and reflect upon how you feel about the pulsation of being close, and then not being so close, and then coming close again, in your new relationship . . .

pause . . . breathe . . . reflect . . . experience

Managing Love

Often the very notion of employing mind-management techniques to help in our love life seems to threaten to take the spontaneity out of the whole experience. After all, sexual passion is supposed to happen by itself, rather than being dictated and controlled by our thinking minds. And I agree, spontaneity is key to successful relating. Where mind management comes to the fore, is when we have habits and attitudes and expectations already ingrained in our minds, that directly interfere with our ability to open up to deeper guidance and freedom of expression.

You've seen that my approach to managing our minds is to use the cognitive tool of reflection to help us choose where we want to focus our mind's attention – and through that choice to manage our minds in directions that in fact encourage deeper intuitive experience and spiritual guidance in our lives. Nowhere is this mind management more needed than in the realm of relating, where if we're not careful our old childhood reactions and negative fear-based emotions can damage or destroy a relationship that otherwise could have flourished.

The relationship meditation I taught in the previous chapter is a good guideline for managing your mind so as to optimize your love life. Let me offer you a few final choices to ponder, as we end this section. Please hold in mind that these aren't necessarily either-or questions, they're focus phrases to evoke deep reflection and insight. Even before you meet the person of your dreams and begin exploring your new relationship, you can begin to reflect upon these primal choices that will strongly influence how your relationship evolves – and be sure to return to a reflection upon these choices, once you do find your true love.

Pause and read each question, then close your eyes, say the question to yourself, see what insights come – and be open to unexpected revelations!

Do you want to jealously possess your new lover, or relate in freedom?

Will you lose your centre in your new lover, or maintain your separate centre?

Do you want to accept your new lover as is, without judgment?

Will your new relationship pulsate between closeness and personal distance?

Do you expect to have to struggle to make your relationship successful?

Are you someone who can live harmoniously with another person?

Are you willing to live with someone who sometimes disagrees with you?

Will you set your lover free to explore his or her own emerging destiny?

What is your vision of a fulfilling long-term relationship?

Can you remain unattached to outcomes in your new relationship?

Will you continue to meditate and nurture your own inner growth?

Do you want to live with your heart and mind centred in love?

And now you can just relax . . . tune into your breathing . . . your heart . . . your whole body here in this present moment . . . and enjoy your present situation . . . let love fill your being . . . enjoy the excitement of what's coming next in your life . . . and allow peace and confidence to smooth out your breathing . . . here and now . . . let love find you!

pause . . . breathe . . . reflect . . . experience

KEEPING THE MAGIC ALIVE

We've now moved through a tremendous amount of exploration together in just one book, and I thank you for being open to the ideas about love and relating that we've discussed. I've been focused on your heart and on doing all we can together here, to make sure you properly prepare for and joyfully attain the deep heart goals you desire. I also thank you for being open to the more spiritual dimensions we've talked about. As the days go by, you'll find that the attraction meditation becomes a very valued mind-management practice that grows more and more exciting each time you pause to move through it.

This book is more a workbook that you return to every day, than a regular text that you read once and put forever aside. In this spirit, I hope you will want to return now to the beginning of the book, and delve more intensely and with more time, into each of the seven steps to finding true love. You'll find that sometimes one of the steps attracts you the most, while on other days another of the steps will most attract you. Please feel free to let your intuition each day guide you towards what you're ready to focus on in this seven-step programme.

Your heart will guide you, if you pause and tune into what it's saying to you. The heart speaks in more subtle ways than the ego mind, but the more you listen with your attention focused lovingly towards your heart, the more you'll be aware of intuitive hunches, subtle yearnings, gentle nudges in important directions. Especially when you quiet your mind in meditation, you'll begin to receive very wonderful guidance from your higher mind and whatever you consider the spiritual dimensions of life. The key is stopping, becoming calm, and focusing within to your heart – then and only then can your higher guidance speak to you, and lead you where you want to go.

So please do return to the beginning chapters and move through the various exercises a number of times – because only through repetition of these primal mind-management techniques do you tap their power to transform how you see life in directions that will serve you. It's the same with the basic attraction meditation in its three time frames – the more you discipline yourself to spend the time and focus your loving attention on saying the focus phrases to yourself, the more you'll benefit!

And do remember that until you find your new lover, you are indeed actively engaged in the hunt of the heart, wherever you are, whatever you're doing. The challenge is to stay quite aware, not to drift off – and to be open to new experience. Just for the fun of it every day, make sure that you spend at least five to ten minutes doing something you've never done before, walking somewhere you've never walked before, talking to someone you've never talked to before, experiencing something new . . . so that your habits loosen up, and you put yourself in new situations where romantic lightning can strike.

Your heart, which is tuned into the presence of your new lover, will guide your feet if you allow your feet the freedom to walk in new directions. Spontaneity is key. You're wanting to encourage the mysterious process of synchronicity in your life – where both you and your new lover let go of habits and open up to spontaneous movements that lead you to your desired encounter. So each moment, breathe freely, let go of rigid plans that tie up every moment of your day – and leave yourself with free time so that you can indeed have new experiences, and unexpected encounters of the heart.

And when you find your true love, I do hope that the short discussions we had in the last section of the book ring true for you. I'm now busy writing a new book on the seeming magic and mind-management logic of creating and sustaining successful relationships, so if you want special discussions and programmes in that direction, we'll meet again soon! And meanwhile do come visit the www.johnselby.com website where there's loads more reading, audio guidance – and the opportunity to meet like-minded folk who've also read this book, and are open to the depth of relating that we've all been exploring here!

Helpful professional guidance such as this book provides is a wonderful thing – I wish I'd had such a book myself when I was struggling to make true love appear in my life in earlier years. But ultimately, even without and certainly beyond all the books and websites and other external guides available, you do already possess what you need most in order to find true love. You possess, as we've explored throughout this book, your very own wise and powerful inner guide – the most positive and loving force in your life. What I've offered are the most effective inner tools for contacting, listening to and responding to that guide, through the attraction meditation and other exercises herein.

So you now have, on all fronts, everything you need to move forward on your own in confidence and power, with hope and faith that the universe does love you, and has a totally wonderful life partner searching right now, for you! Just hold in mind constantly until that person appears, that your own prevailing attitudes about being successful in your hunt will ultimately determine the outcome of that hunt. Your success in properly managing the thoughts and emotions you choose to let dominate your mind will prove the key factor that allows true love to find you.

Each and every moment, you and only you can choose to hold negative thoughts in your mind that make your search feel hopeless – or hold positive thoughts in your mind that enable you to feel attractive, headed towards love, and determined to find that true love you so desire. So relax, take time to master the attraction meditations – and allow the programmes in this book to help you move in directions that nurture your soul and bring fulfilling love into your life.

Blessings on your inner adventure, enjoy the thrill of the hunt, luxuriate in your coming encounter – and dedicate yourself to your magnificent new relationship!

HEART-TO-HEART COMMUNITY

Naturally, a book such as this stands entirely on its own as a complete presentation of the methods being taught. However, very often with all my books, readers also value additional online support in related themes and methods, to augment programmes they're learning from the book. Therefore I also encourage you to explore our free online teaching and inspirational communities where you can read author updates and consider further dimensions of this 'let love find you' mind-management theme, and also delve into related themes and methods. Through feeling that you belong to a community of people exploring the same techniques and life experiences, a special sense of heart-warming community comes into being which can be of vital help in encouraging your success with the programmes and aims of this book. So do feel free to drop in and visit me at www.johnselby.com anytime, and see what's happening that's of value to you.

Online Audio Guidance and Support

In reading through this book the first time, you've had a taste of the various guided meditations and experiences that make up the actual training of the attraction-meditation programme. For years before the internet was invented, I would record cassette programmes so that people could listen to my voice guiding them through the meditations and inner exercises of a book. Now you can go to the Singles Section of my website and listen to the guided-audio versions of the various meditations in this book so that you learn them by heart. There is also a complete in-depth online course to enjoy, if you want day-by-day multi-media guidance through this learning process, plus loads of extra support.

You can also read related discussions that I post on the website; ask me questions via email (in English please) which I'll respond to; and participate in online forums where we all offer our insights and experiences related to a particular theme. Furthermore, you can read a number of my other books online, and listen to a wide variety of guided audio sessions and meditations to further your general emotional healing and spiritual exploration.

Meeting Each Other Online

As funding allows, I am posting a special 'Heart-To-Heart' Singles Encounter system on my website, where you and all other people reading this book can go online, fill out a special personality questionnaire based on the premises of this book, and begin to meet like-minded folk who might end up becoming a special friend or even your life mate.

A special magic does come into being when two people happen to buy and read the same book at the same time, and move through the same mind-management process – then begin to relate with each other with this common bond of walking the same path at the same time. In this spirit, I want to offer you an effective way to meet each other online, and enable the synchronistic magic of encounter to act through the internet medium. So go to www.johnselby.com and the Singles button, and check it out! You might also note when 'Let Love Find You' weekend seminars are being offered near you!

Attraction-Meditation Training CDs

For those of you without online computers, and those who want to receive audio training in these attraction meditations away from your computer, you can order the primary 'Let Love Find You' CD by mail. Please go online to the CD STORE section of my website, where you can use your credit card from anywhere in the world to order your own CD. You can also send $12 plus $4 handling and shipping ($6 from outside the USA) to: Let Love Find You CD, PO Box 861, Kilauea HI 967854. Make cheques payable to John Selby.

Source Books and Further Reading
There are numerous related books that I will list and discuss online, so that you can learn more specific information and techniques about the various themes and programmes of this book. We'll also be hosting video interviews with people you'll find extremely insightful and helpful as you progress on your journey to heart fulfilment.

ATTRACTION MEDITATION –

Final Review

O nce you've studied the various dimensions of this book in depth, you can quickly gain the overview by turning to this final section – and moving every day through this somewhat shorter version of the basic heart-attraction process.

◆ Make sure you're feeling comfortable – feel free to stretch all you want, and yawn . . . let your body move as it wants, to discharge tensions.

◆ Tune into the air flowing in and out your nose . . . expand your awareness to include the movements in your chest and belly . . . and gently expand your awareness to include the feelings in your heart . . .

◆ Accept whatever feelings you find right now, breathe into them, let them change with each new breath . . .

◆ Expand your awareness to include your whole body, here in this present moment. Be aware of your toes . . . your hands . . . your throat . . . your pelvis . . . your knees . . . your belly . . . find places that feel especially good right now . . . enjoy the good feelings you find . . .

◆ Bring your focus to your breathing again . . . the feelings in your heart . . . and think of someone you love. Let your love for this person fill your heart as you aim your attention towards this person – they will feel your attention . . . they can feel your love . . . enjoy this heart-to-heart communion . . .

◆ And now shift into receive mode in your heart, so that you begin to feel the love this person has for you . . . open your heart, and let their love come in . . .

◆ And open your heart to receive the pure spiritual love of the universe . . . with every new breath, be open to receive more love, until your whole heart and being fills with love . . .

◆ And now, gently return your attention to your breaths, coming and going . . . and begin to say the following focus phrases that will awaken new experience in your heart, mind and soul . . ._

1. Yearning
. . . after saying each of these focus phrases, pause and see how you feel in your heart, about the intent you just stated:

'I want to heal my emotional wounds . . .'
'I feel a deep yearning for new love . . .'
'I am going to attract new love to me . . .'

~ pause & experience ~

2. Forgiving and Healing
. . . let go . . . accept . . . forgive . . . open up and receive healing and love . . . say your intent . . . experience the reverberations of the words . . .

'I accept and love myself, just as I am.'
'I forgive and let go of my old lovers.'
'My heart is open to receive . . . healing . . . and love.'

~ pause & experience ~

3. Waking Up Sexually

You are as beautiful as you feel inside . . . let yourself feel good . . . let the world see you as attractive and powerful and full of love . . .

'I am a beautiful powerful sexual being.'
'I give myself permission to feel good in my body.'
'See me – sexually attractive . . . ready for love.'

~ pause & experience ~

4. Charging

. . . focus specifically on the passion you feel inside your body, in your heart, in your belly, in your genitals, in your throat – in your whole body. Say the statements one by one . . . breathe . . . and pause to experience whatever new feelings and insights come to you . . .

'I feel passion . . . in my heart . . . in my belly . . .'
'I feel sexual hunger in my genitals . . . in my throat . . .'
'My whole being is charged with loving energy.'

~ pause & experience ~

5. Broadcasting

. . . let the world know you're here and you're ready for your true love. Say it – do it! Let these words empower you . . . wake up the world to your desire . . . and aim your intent directly towards that person out there who is also aiming towards you . . .

'Here I am right now, yearning for love.'
'I am reaching out to you . . .'
'Feel me . . . come into my life.'

~ pause & experience ~

6. Surrendering

... allow your thoughts to become quiet ... your breathing even and deep ... and go ahead and ask for help and guidance ... open your entire being to the greater loving force that will bring your heart together with your lover-to-be ...

'My mind is quiet ... my breathing calm.'
'I request help from my deeper source.'
'I surrender to spiritual wisdom and guidance.'

~ pause & experience ~

7. Moving Towards Encounter

... now go all the way ... open up to experience connection with your lover ... say it ... experience it ... from the depths of your heart, say the following statements ... pause after each one ... breathe ... experience ...

'I let go of inhibitions ...'
'I need you ... I love you ...'
'Here I am – I feel you!'

~ pause & experience ~

◆ ... just relax ... stay with your feelings ... allow your breaths to deepen ... and as you hold your heart open to your new lover, feel in your whole body what this person is like ... as if you are already in your lover's arms ... look deeply into your lover's eyes ... see your lover's soul ... you are together already in spirit ...

◆ .You can stay in meditation for as long as you want ... and when you're ready you can open your eyes ... stretch and yawn ... and as you go about your day, be spontaneous in where you go ... so that your two bodies can move closer and closer towards each other ... let spirit move you through your day ... as you come closer to suddenly encountering each other ... looking into each other's eyes ... and knowing – that you have found your true love!

pause ... breathe ... reflect ... experience

John Selby is a psychologist, writer, counsellor and leading relationships expert, whose tried-and-tested techniques have already helped thousands of people to find their perfect partner. He studied at Princeton and UC Berkeley, and did mind research at the US National Institute of Health and the Bureau of Research in Neurology and Psychiatry. He teaches and leads seminars in both America and Europe, and is the author of over two dozen highly acclaimed books, including *Seven Masters, One Path* and *Quiet Your Mind*. He is the innovator of experiential online training courses, and lives in Hawaii and California. You can reach John at www.johnselby.com.

Also by John Selby:

Jesus for the Rest of Us
Quiet Your Mind
Seven Masters, One Path
Conscious Healing
Finding Each Other
Shattering Jade
Sex and Spirit
Secrets of a Good Night's Sleep
Fathers: Opening Up
Immune System Activation
Enjoying Solitude
Peak Sexual Experience
The Visual Handbook
Couples Massage
Powerpoint